The Dressage Formula

With best wishes,
Jackie, for many
interesting and enjoy-
able hours in the
saddle!

Yours sincerely

Nik

.... and plenty of carrots for Smokey!

ERIK F. HERBERMANN

The Dressage Formula

Foreword by Egon von Neindorff

J.A. ALLEN

LONDON · NEW YORK

First published 1980
Reprinted 1984
Reprinted 1986

British Library Cataloguing in Publication Data

Herbermann, Erik F.
  The dressage formula.
  1. Dressage
  I. Title
  636.1′8′186   SF309.5

ISBN 0–85131–348–5

Published by
J. A. Allen & Company Limited,
1, Lower Grosvenor Place, Buckingham Palace Road,
London, SW1W 0EL

Printed and bound in Great Britain by
The Garden City Press Limited,
Letchworth, Hertfordshire

Contents

Functions of the basic natural tools in the giving of aids. The seat. Inside leg and outside rein. Outside leg and inside rein. What function does the hand play? The voice. Spurs and crop. The correct attitude and driving influence from the seat.
Incorrect attitudes and driving influence of the seat and position.
What is a weight aid?
Timing of the driving aid from the legs.
Important factors about activating the horse.
Tuning the horse to aids from seat and legs.
Quality of the rein contact.
Quality, quantity and intonation of the aids.
Sequence of changing position and aids when changing the rein.
REFLECTIONS

Preface

WITHIN the covers of this book is an organized documentation of ideals and standards of fundamental academic dressage riding. In words and pictures are summarized the findings of a meticulous and critical study of the long-established principles of horsemanship, which I have diligently applied and tested in both training and instructing.

This work does not pretend to be a replacement for the excellent literature written by the Great Masters. The basic concept is by no means new. The reason for this book is primarily to be a concise theoretical support for the hour of instruction or personal riding sessions; leaving these free to be fully utilized for their rightful purpose . . . the translation of theory into practice.

The emphasis of the text is singularly aimed at accuracy, brevity, clarity and objectivity. The headings of all sections are numbered for the purpose of cross-reference, to avoid tedious repetition or redundancy.

I sincerely hope that this guideline will be of some assistance to all dedicated scholars of horsemanship.

ERIK F. HERBERMANN
Uxbridge, September 1978

Vorwort

HERR Erik Herbermann hat in seinen mehrjärigen Aufenthalten an meinem Karlsruher Institut nicht nur reiterliches Können gezeigt. In einer Zeit des schnellen Wechsels und ständiger "Umwertung der Werte" bewies Herbermann Klarheit und ungewöhnliches Einfülungsvermögen mit der Beständigkeit, die seine Arbeitsweise auszeichnet. Das kam der erfreulichen Fülle fachlicher Kenntniss und praktischer Erfahrung sehr zugute, die in seinem Buch niedergelegt sind.

Die anschauliche Art der Darstellung, erläutert mit vielen instruktiven Bildaufnahmen aus der Arbeit des Autors, spricht den Leser als Freund der gemeinsamen Sache ebenso an wie die Probleme der täglichen Praxis. Sorgsamer Aufbau der Ausbildung von Pferd und Reiter ist der Grundzug dieses Bekenntnisses zur reellen, dauerhaften und vielseitigen Basis reiterlicher Erfolge.

So wünsche ich diesem Buch weite Verbreitung bei allen, denen die Probleme der Reiterei unserer Zeit mit Ernst am Herzen liegen.

EGON VON NEINDORFF

Foreword (translation)

DURING his many years' stay at my Riding Institution in Karlsruhe, Mr. Erik Herbermann has not only displayed equestrian ability. In an age of rapid changes and continual 'alteration of the values', Herbermann demonstrated a clarity and unusual perception for constancy which distinguish his method of work. This has come to good stead in the gratifying abundance of professional knowledge and practical experience which have been laid down in his book.

The intuitive mode of presentation, which is illustrated by many instructive photographs of the author's work, relates to the reader as a friend both about general matters as well as the problems of daily practice. Careful construction in the training of horse and rider is the characteristic of this Creed for a real, enduring and diverse basis of equestrian successes.

Thus I wish this book a wide propagation to all those who seriously take to heart the problems of riding in our times.

EGON VON NEINDORFF

11

Acknowledgements

I WOULD like to thank my instructors and friends who have contributed significantly to my education both as a person and as a horseman. I wish to include special recognition to those who have generously spent caring hours during my 'early years'. Often such individuals are overlooked because they are not amongst the "world's renowned masters". I recognize, however, that without their patient guidance, at a time when I could have hardly been considered anything other than a stumbling beginner, I would not have arrived at this somewhat more advanced stage in horsemanship.

Initially, I had the opportunity to study with Mrs. Patricia Salt, FBHS., who taught with precision and correctness, to the letter, the art of riding that she herself had learned at the Spanish Riding School. She was also a student of Mr. R.L. Wätjen. Others who helped me during these stages were: Walter Thiessen, Heidi Hannibal and Monty Smith. It was through Dietrich von Hopffgarten that I was accepted at the Reitinstitut von Neindorff in Karlsruhe. I was greatly influenced by Mr. von Hopffgarten's riding, and most grateful for his contribution of an explicit example of fine horsemanship which radiated such undeniable qualities of competence and truth.

I am particularly deeply indebted to Mr. Egon von Neindorff from whom I have been able to glean the bulk of material upon which I have built my training and instructing experiences. It has been a unique education to work under the close personal guidance of this knowledgeable, artistic Master.

Thanks to Mr. Dan A'haroni for the generous assistance given in directing me to the publisher of this work. I would also like to extend further gratitude to both Mr. A'haroni and Mr. John Pullen for the contribution they have made to this book in offering their frank constructive criticism and advice.

Many thanks to Jaqueline Johnson for the hours spent in typing the manuscript; and to both Joan Smith and Lindsay Shanahan for their assistance in editing the text. The X-ray shots were made possible through the kind assistance of Mr. & Mrs. Kenneth Giles, and the capable hands of Miss Janice Kneider, and Dr. N. Brown, Chief Radiologist. I would like to extend special thanks to Mrs. V. Boynton who has most generously supported me during these years in the establishing of the fine school facilities.

Finally, I wish to express my appreciation to Mr. J.A. Allen, and to the professionals of the J.A. Allen Company for the special care they have taken to produce this publication so beautifully.

All photographs are by George A. Ross.

14

AN INTRODUCTION TO THE HORSES IN THIS BOOK

THE horses that have been used to illustrate the text are all of the common 'back-yard' variety. The different breeds represented vary considerably in size, conformation, movement and temperament. Horses that have naturally good gaits, and which are naturally well balanced, offer the rider a great deal, and lessen the training problems immeasurably. For the rider who is capable, however, it is always interesting to work with equine material which is far from ideal, and carefully construct an end-product which is both pleasing to ride and to observe. When the basic motion of horses such as these can be substantially improved, it stands as an irrefutable witness to the validity of effective practical gymnastics.

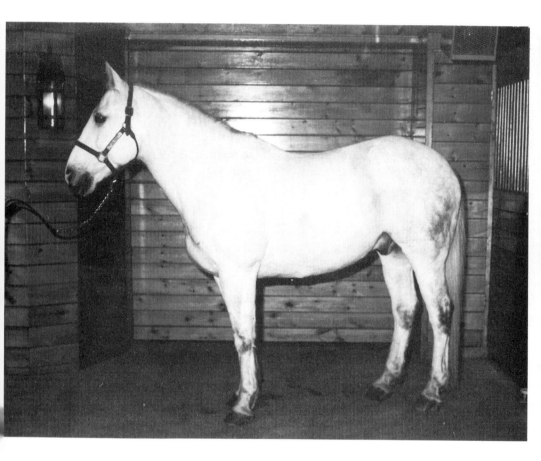

ATLANTIS

Grey gelding. Born 1966. Percheron-thoroughbred cross. $16\frac{1}{2}$"hh. (164 cm). By nature he is a poor mover, his gaits are 'klunky'. Re-training this fellow to become active, supple and obedient was like schooling a heavy-weight wrestler to do Ballet! It proved to be an interesting and challenging task. Atlantis started his training with the Author at the age of 10. He was previously used as a family 'hack', and was also occasionally hunted.

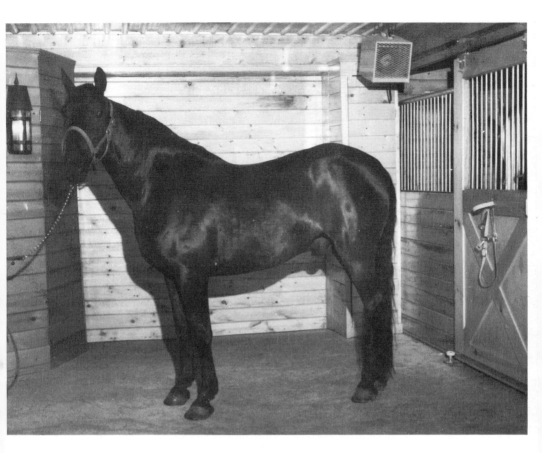

METEORITE

Dark brown gelding. Standardbred and cross bred (?). Born (est.)
1963. 15-3½"hh. (161.5 cm). Before being purchased by the Author
(1976) he had gone the 'severe-bit route', and was quite thoroughly
ruined. His body was knotted with tensions. It has taken over two
years to PARTIALLY resolve the problems. This horse is represented in the book to demonstrate the interesting and valuable
examples of how tensions manifest themselves in the gaits. Also an
elucidating series portrays improvements of the extended trot over a
period of 18 months. He is by far the most athletic mover of these
three horses.

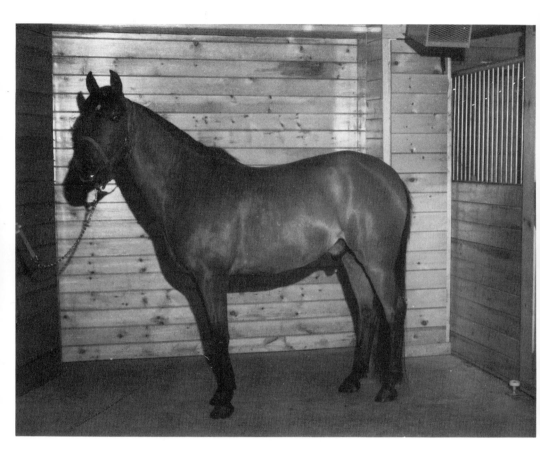

HAWTHORN'S BARGEL
(Barty)

Bay gelding. Born 1971. $\frac{3}{4}$ Arab – $\frac{1}{4}$ Pony. 14-2″hh (147.5 cm). He has a flat 'Daisy-cutter' motion, with a dash of the choppy Pony gait added. His jaw-throat-jowl area is tight and fleshy, therefore the 'forward and downward' exercises are demonstrated with him (which is an excellent exercise for horses with this particular conformation problem.) He is a very willing little chap!

THE DEFINITION OF DRESSAGE*

DRESSAGE is the methodical, gymnastic training of the horse. It is based upon the three natural gaits – walk, trot and canter, which must be carefully cultivated and improved through disciplined work. With this training the horseman attempts, while working his horse under saddle, to maintain the balanced beauty and harmonious movement that is found in the 'untampered-with horse'.

When correctly implemented, dressage is above all a practical obedience training which prolongs the animal's usefulness and makes it a pleasure to ride. All forms of exercises, regardless of difficulty, including the highschool airs above the ground, find their roots in the same movements in raw form in nature.

*SYNONYMS for the word 'DRESSAGE'

- Work on the flat (This term used in jumping)
- English Riding
- Training by the Natural Method
- Academic Riding (encompasses the next two disciplines)
- Highschool Riding (advanced work)
- The Art of Classical Riding (dressage in it's ultimate form)

The Author with Atlantis.

CHAPTER I

A GUIDELINE FOR THE MENTAL PREPARATION OF THE RIDER

002

WHAT DOES THE ACTUAL RIDING TASK ENTAIL?

THE horse already knows how to be a horse. The task of horsemanship lies entirely with the rider. Through training the horse, the rider must gain accurate control over all the various movements which the horse can already perform naturally, and improve on the basic motion, through disciplined gymnastic work.

It is the prime duty of the true horseman to be strictly a control-centre; not a physical mover, shover or pusher-puller of the animal. This state can only materialize when the rider, through consequential, consistent use of his aids, establishes a system of communication, causing the horse to understand what is wanted.

The only physical responsibility to be mastered by the rider is that he becomes entirely an inseparable part of the horse, in no way disturbing its body movements.

003

WHY ARE SO MANY YEARS REQUIRED TO LEARN CORRECT RIDING?

A lengthy learning process is required because the riding is like an intangible phantom. It is continuously mobile and plastic. Its proportions cannot be measured or weighed.

Two living creatures, each on entirely different physical and mental planes, attempt to become united. The unique character of each horse and personality of each rider, compounded with their own individual physical variations and problems, comprise almost limitless combinations that must be dealt with in order to construct an end result in which the rider's mind does the thinking, and the horse's body does the doing.

To attain this goal, one must engage in a serious, intensive study, spanning over many years; closely adhering to the guidelines which have been established by the great masters over the past centuries, and fulfilling these theoretical principles through practical application within one's daily work.

004
AN ELABORATION OF PRACTICAL MENTAL ATTITUDES

1. To participate in the Academic form of Dressage riding, the horseman must become fastidiously self-critical and cultivate a refined degree of mental self-control. The rider must also be sufficiently mature and disciplined to be able to realistically assess and compile the results of his performance.
2. The rider must become well acquainted with the psychological and physical nature of the horse. Through our instructors we are to learn how to 'read the horse' so that we can recognize the signs and signals which are to be the guidelines by which we should allow ourselves to be led, in order to influence the animal favourably. The horse will accurately mirror our ability, character, and favourable as well as undesirable attributes. (026, 057, 058).
3. It is entirely the duty of each rider to work diligently if he wishes to reach high equestrian standards. No matter how good the instructor or horses may be, unless the student is open-minded and receptive, only a relatively mediocre level will ever be attained.
4. The horse is in no way interested in our personal ambitions. Only when the rider has the correct combination, of appropriate mental attitudes and an adequately clear administration of his aids, will the horse readily comply.
5. It is the horseman's complete and sole responsibility, being the more intelligent, to find logical solutions to all problems within himself. There are always reasons . . . never excuses.
6. There is only one kind of mistake, that is, the FUNDAMEN-TAL mistake. Regardless of how advanced the exercise, if the

performance is defective, one can directly trace that fault to a lack in the fundamental training of either the horse or the rider.

7. The chief motivator of our attitudes should be a love for the horses. When this theme encompasses all our intentions it fosters the humility and learning attitude which aid the rider to persevere through the difficulties encountered on the road to discovering the horse.

8. We must learn to distinguish between a 'judicious leadership' needed to guide the horse with firmness and persistence, and an 'arrogant dictatorship' which is enforced through the thoughtless subjugation of the animal.

9. We should come to recognize our own limitations, thereby not demanding work from the horse that we ourselves are incapable of controlling. Out of this self-acceptance we will learn to gain enjoyment from small daily successes. It is far too seldom appreciated what a mammoth task dressage riding assigns to the horseman; therefore we see so frequently riders over-facing their horses and themselves, and inadvertently having to resort to force, 'home-baked' aids and trickery, in order to produce SUPPOSED results.

10. The process of the rider's own learning often goes at considerable expense to the horses. The animals experience great contradictions before the rider learns how to administer and coordinate his aids correctly; all of which the horses generally endure with great patience and good humour. A sympathy and compassion for the horses should therefore rule, despite the rider's own frustrations and tribulations.

11. The rider can only become an effective critic of his own work once he comes to know what the necessary criterion is. UNDERSTANDING IS THE KEY TO MEANINGFUL PRACTICE. Much time is required, under close guidance, to learn to recognize all the fine nuances which differentiate the academic form of riding from artificial, trick or circus methods. Much can be learned (positively and negatively) from observing others ride, provided we remain objective in our criticism (having a truly studious attitude), and being empathetic with the

person we are judging.

12. A close rapport between man and mount is the backbone of good horsemanship. The rider must respect the horse's physical strength, and with the utmost of care regard its nature. The horse is to learn to respect and obey its intellectually superior master. The rider, however, must EARN this respect through fair, consistent handling, discreetly utilizing praise and correction.

13. It is essential to develop an extended concentration span. Decisions must be instant, both in handling from the ground or during riding. The rider's control is largely dependent on preparation or prevention since the horse's reactions are many times faster than Man's. Through the rider's ability to prepare both himself and his horse, an element of predictability gells between the human and animal partners . . . the nucleus of a smooth performance.

14. If the horse becomes frightened and shies, or when it has suddenly been startled, our attitudes and reactions should be those which will maintain the horse's confidence in us. It would be a mistake to pull the horse about and become angry because this would only confirm in the horse's mind that there was truly something to be frightened of. Instead, the rider should ignore that which is exciting or frightening the animal, and with a nonchalant air DECISIVELY urge the horse to continue-on with the task at hand (if necessary use a reassuring voice). The rider must learn to become a strong, reliable and just leader . . . a kind, firm guiding force.

15. Punishment.
    (a)   When should one resort to punishment?
          Considerable experience and understanding is required to determine whether punishment is actually warranted. The following points should certainly be taken into account: Were the aids correct and clear? Is the horse capable of executing the work being asked of it (over-facing)? Lastly, is it a clear case of disobedience?

(b) How to punish fairly.

If it is determined that the horse must be punished, it should be done quickly and methodically, not out of ill-temperedness or lack of self-control, venting one's frustrations on the animal. Usually a few smart whacks with the stick, or a decisive, emphatic aid with the spurs is more than adequate. Under certain circumstances, a stern voice aid can suffice in re-establishing one's authority. If the horse is not punished immediately after the misdemeanour is committed it will not understand why it was punished.

(c) How much punishment is necessary?

The type and amount of punishment should be carefully suited to the character and sensitivity of the horse, and proportionate to the severity of the infraction.

(d) The 'Come-back'. What to do after correction has been made.

This last stage is essential to success but is a factor which is often neglected; reaffirming continued friendship and confidence. Once the correction has been made, do not linger on the matter, proceed immediately with a fresh start and reward the horse for even the slightest signs of co-operation. In this way the horse will readily learn that compliance with the rider's requests is rewarded with kindness and praise, but that disobedience is met with unpleasant reactions.

16. We must always work with a clear purpose in mind, (the accurate riding of school figures and a disciplined, meaningful choice of exercises. 040–043). Aimless riding teaches neither us nor the horse anything.

17. The rider should end his work with an exercise that the horse can do easily, just to finish on a happy note.

18. In order to complete the mosaic of horsemanship, it is important

that the background-scene is conducive to the safety, comfort and peace of mind of the horses.

Rough, indifferent handling causes the horses to become distrustful and frightened, or makes them into the unpredictable rogues that acquire obnoxious habits of biting or kicking. Only if they are cared for with conscientious, quiet work and thoughtful handling while mucking-out, grooming and generally cleaning the stables, will the horses settle down and be in a good frame of mind, and therefore be well prepared for their work in the manège.

REFLECTIONS I

- Armed with theory, practice becomes meaningful . . . through practice, theory becomes fulfilled.
- An important, sizeable portion of the riding task lies in coming to grips with oneself.
- To achieve uniform results, the rider must become the equalizing entity which compensates for the variations between horses.
8 Putting the horse to work precludes many of the shying or silliness problems.
- Every master has his horse.
- Rider's tact and feel cannot be taught . . . it is for each individual to develop these within himself.
- Dressage is the fundamental obedience training . . . for the rider!
- Each day brings its improvements or regressions; its new problems and challenges; its defeats and victories . . . the learning process is never done.
- As one comes to a deeper understanding of the horse's psychology, the more it is discovered, to one's chagrin, how dependent the rider is upon the horse's generosity.
- Patience. . . .

26

Atlantis. Ordinary walk. The correct position and seats is the basis for a clear, effective dialogue with the horse.

Meteorite. Working trot.

CHAPTER II

THE RIDER'S SEAT AND POSITION

005
PHYSICAL ATTITUDES

WITHIN the physical attitudes we encompass the modes of the rider's position and seat. Though it takes many years of diligent work to gain the necessary independence and control of individual body parts, the physical attributes are, nonetheless, considerably less important than the mental ones. Physical problems, outside major bodily incapacitation, can all be brought under control and can somehow be compensated for.

The rider's hips and seat, and thigh down to the knee, and his hand and forearm to the elbow, become part of the horse entirely. The only physical parts of the rider which remain his own are his head and upper body, and upper arm to the elbow, and his lower legs. The supple controlling links between these two categories are:
THE LOWER BACK, the lumbar vertebrae, acting as the chief controlling factor through which all aids are transferred to the horse.
THE SUPPLE SHOULDERS, which act as a buffer to the horse's mouth.

It is imperative that the position is well stretched at all times; the upper body growing taller, and the rider's weight directed through lowered heels towards the ground (imagine making grooves in the ground with both heels). This attitude allows the concentration of weight to fall clearly into the seat.

Though correctness of the position is of great importance, one must not lose sight of the over-riding need to remain thoroughly supple within this correctness. Involuntary tensions in the rider hamper the clarity and influence of the aids, and restrict the freedom of movement in the horse's back, adversely affecting the purity of the gaits. The good position and seat has an athletically controlled tension or 'tune', completely void of stiffness or contortion.

006

THE FIVE MAJOR POSITION CORRECTIONS[1]

- Head up
- Chest out[2]
- Fists vertical
- Knees closed
- Heels deep

The position corrections must be kept in as simple a form as possible, so that they are easy to remember during the riding sessions. Simplicity of the work load, that is, staying with one theme, is extremely important to actually acquiring any new physical attribute.

If after having taken instruction the individual has other corrections to make pertaining specifically to himself, then these should be added, also in simple form, after the basic five. No seat or position will improve without the continuous mental repetition of these points, followed by the immediate physical correction.

007

THE SEAT

THE seat is comprised of two major parts, 50% is formed by the rider, the other 50% is made up by the horse. However, both of these equal portions are entirely the responsibility of the rider. To be realistic, the sad fact needs to be stated that unless the rider is capable of causing his horse to carry him on an elastic back, a good seat cannot be cultivated. In other words, only the combined correctness of the rider's seat and position elastically balanced upon the supple, natural motion of the horse can consummate the true unity. In order to cultivate a 'good seat', one must acquire a very thorough knowledge of the whole horse.

---

[1] Egon von Neindorff.

[2] Lengthen the front or stomach line; and/or shoulder blades together. Take care, however, not to hollow the lower back!

008

CORRECT POSITION AND ATTITUDE OF THE SEAT (also see 019)

1. THE RIDER MUST SIT IN THE DEEPEST PART OF THE SADDLE, with the seat having the attitude of being held into the front of the saddle.
2. SIT MAINLY ON THE SEAT BONES, however, one should also be partially supported by the pelvic structure which lies between and in front of the two seatbones.
3. EQUAL WEIGHT ON BOTH SEAT BONES. (Except when riding on circles, bent lines, or position right or left, and two-track work, in which case the inside seatbone must have a bit more weight on it.) 021, 027/1.
4. SIT SQUARELY IN THE SADDLE. (Do not collapse onto one hip.)
5. THE HIPS MUST BE HELD PARALLEL TO THE HORSE'S HIPS. (While riding on bent lines the rider's inside hip is brought forward.)
6. THE BUTTOCK MUSCLES MUST BE RELAXED AND OPENED, in conjunction with well-turned thighs.

009

THE SHOULDERS

– The shoulders must be kept level. Common faults are:–
   (a)   One shoulder carried higher.
   (b)   The inside shoulder held ahead of the outside one (skiing position).
– While riding on bent lines, the outside shoulder must be brought forward somewhat (shoulders parallel to horse's shoulders).
– A helpful exercise to find the correct shoulder position is:–
   Move the shoulders all the way . . . forward and down . . . forward and up . . . up and back . . . back and down. (an upside-down 'U').

31

UPPER LEG AND KNEE POSITION

ONLY a correct leg position and attitude will allow the rider to sit clearly on his seat bones. The thigh must be turned completely inward from the hip joint, combined with an actual drawing-back of the thigh muscle, out from underneath the femur. This results not only in the correct opening of the seat muscles, but also allows the knees to come in a holding contact with the saddle. Needing to have the knees closed, should not be translated into a clamping-on or unnecessary gripping. The thigh muscle should lie relaxed on the saddle. The upper leg, to the knee, should point quite strongly to the ground. The knees should be brought back as far as possible, however, not so far that the rider begins to sit on his thighs (fork or crotch seat). If the knees are too high, the rider cannot effectively bring his weight into his seat and through to the ground (chair seat).

011

LOWER LEG AND FOOT POSITION

THESE are the main points:–

(a) When observing the rider from the side, the heel should be on the vertical line through the centre of the rider's shoulder and hip.
  – leg aids are more effectively given from this position.
  – The rider is better able to balance himself.
(b) The foot should run almost parallel to the horse's sides. This attitude helps prevent the following problems:–
  – Sitting on the thighs.
  – Clamping-on with the lower leg.
  – Digging at the horse with the heels.
(c) Together with a relaxed ankle joint, the heel must be the lowest point of the rider. (This is an end result of correct sitting)
  – Helps draw the weight into the seat.
  – The calf muscle is thereby tensed, a more accurate aid can be given.

(d) The lower leg should always be in a holding contact with the horse. (The lower leg breathes with the horse). It should be as quiet as possible. It may wave slightly with the motion of the horse's body. An exaggerated, incessant tapping is to be avoided.

012

THE ARMS

THE arms hang from relaxed, drawn-back shoulders. The upper arms lie lightly by the rider's sides. The lower arm and fist should be on the straight line from the bit to the elbow. Both the wrist and elbow should always be supple and relaxed. The wrist may not be broken. The back of the hand, and the forearm must form a smooth continuous line.

Mistakes to be watched for:–
   – Stiff out-stretched arms
   – Broken wrists
   – Hands which are boring downward, or too high
   – Stiffness in the shoulder, elbow or writs

013

THE FISTS

BOTH fists should be held at the same height. The fists must be held vertically, the thumbs uppermost. This is an extremely important requirement, for it has been discovered that with this position the hand is the most sensitive and articulate; giving it the most liberty to move as directed by the horse's way of going. The hand must be perfectly quiet in relationship to the horse's mouth. From this comes the old saying:– "The hand stands still, but moves anyway." The hand's attitude should always be 'alive' (feeling), never stark, hard or unfriendly.

33

014
HEAD POSITION

THE head must be held upright, since only in this attitude can the weight of our entire upper body fall correctly into the seat. Keep in mind, that a hanging head nullifies the driving ability of the seat. Also to be avoided is the tipping of the head left or right, especially during work on bent lines. One should, by and large, direct one's vision over the horse's head. Do not stick the chin out in front; keep it somewhat drawn-in. Keep the head quiet . . . DO NOT NOD.

015
CRITERION FOR CORRECT RISING TROT

- The rider has a mobile centre of balance which moves between the knee and seat.
- The inclination of the upper body is directly related to the centre of balance and velocity of the horse. In extended work the inclination will be somewhat more forward, as opposed to the collected work in which the upper body becomes almost vertical. Should the horse be rushing, then the upper body must be brought well forward to coincide with the horse's centre of balance, only then can the horse effectively be brought back-down in rhythm.
- The horse should move the rider; it isn't necessary to stand up forcibly.
- The motion of the seat should be forward and back (hips through the elbows), as opposed to an exaggerated upward motion.
- The 'rise' should be small.
- Rise as the horse's outside front leg goes forward (remember to switch when changing the rein, to exercise both diagonals equally).
- The 'sit' is the most important, it is the moment we activate the horse. A non-sitting, 'hovering' over the saddle is incorrect. However, do not drop or fall into the horse's back when coming to sit.
- Care must be taken to rise and sit squarely, to avoid a twisting and mincing motion of either seat or shoulders.

34

- The knee and lower leg are stationary. The knee acts as a pivot.
- The leg and toe must be well turned in.
- The rider's weight should go clearly into his heels at each stride, showing a dip each time the rider rises.
- The hands are to be ABSOLUTELY MOTIONLESS (no exceptions). This, however, does not mean rigid!

REFLECTIONS II

- The seat is the alpha and omega of the riding. (Egon von Neindorff)
- The hands must remain, strictly, each on its own side of the horse's neck.
- It is a serious fault to be sitting in the back of the saddle, being pushed along by the cantle.
- If the rider has continuously got his heels drawn up, his seat is fundamentally incorrect.
- Remember to let the horse do the work; the rider is only the control centre.
- Always make a clear distinction in leg position when bending the horse or changing the rein (outside leg well back 027).
- The seat cannot be cultivated as an isolated entity; its quality is directly related to the correctness of its influence on the horse.
- An artificial, superficial position, without seat, is worthless. A good seat, without an athletically good position, is impossible.
- The hands are only as good as the seat.
- The rider can sit over the horse – on the horse – or IN the horse. The last of these is the ultimate goal.
- The hand is ideal only once it becomes a 'receiving agent', as opposed to being an active, positive entity.
- All leg aids must be given from a closed knee.
- Too high a hand position robs the horse of the use of its back, and snubs off the impulsion from behind.

Atlantis. Shortened working canter right (see footnotes 035).

36

CHAPTER III

THE AIDS

TO gain the fullest possible benefit from the contents of this chapter, it is essential that the reader does not succumb to the fallacy of believing that there is a simple, stark method to the administration of aids. One also must not isolate any one factor within this chapter; it is only through the sum-total of combined facets described, that a full and competent giving of aids can evolve. . . . The Symphony of Aids.

The quality of the aids (or lack of same) is in direct relation to the skill and experience of the rider. The less experienced rider still needs to use relatively coarse, obvious aids; the advanced rider can tune the horse so finely that response is attained from mere suggestions.

While learning to implement the elements put forth in the following pages, it is important to go ahead and 'just ride', and only gradually introduce these aspects so as not to become so entangled in theory, that one can no longer "see the riding for the aids."

016
DEFINITION OF THE AIDS

(a)   Aids are the vocabulary of riding.
(b)   They must be short and accurate; a MOMENTARY adjustment of the horse.
(c)   Be decisive, GET A RESULT. (Aimless badgering only dulls horses).
(d)   When the result comes, INSTANTLY STOP giving the aid. (Neutralize the hand, leg or seat).
(e)   CONTRAST is the strength and clarity of the aid!

PRINCIPLES IN THE GIVING OF AIDS

(a)   The driving aids far exceed the receiving or restraining aids of the hands.

(b)   Work the horse from back to front. (Never pull the horse together by the reins).

(c)   Never use an active rein aid without using a supporting passive leg aid, and/or appropriate weight aid.

(d)   Only use ONE active aid at any one time; the other aids being passive and holding (supporting).

(e)   All aids must work together towards one single intention. (No contradictory aids).

(f)   Equal pressure in both legs; except when giving a sideways-yielding aid.

(g)   Equal pressure in both reins; except when giving a bending aid.

Split-second correct timing in administering aids or praise and correction, is of the utmost of importance to achieving successful reactions from the horse.

The aids are not to be a monologue, blindly thundering from the rider. One must become subject to (and allow oneself to be directed by) the horse. The aids must be carefully suited to the degree of training, temperament and sensitivity of each individual horse.

An indispensable factor to improved riding lies in the cultivation of one's sensitivity. Only when we can feel a result from our aids will the horse begin to react to them.

FUNCTIONS OF THE BASIC NATURAL TOOLS IN THE GIVING OF AIDS

The prime function of the natural riding tools (seat, hands, and legs) is to PASSIVELY contain, form, hold, and support the horse. From this neutral, passive state the basic tools perform specific functions which are stipulated below.

THE SEAT:–   All aids find their basis in or act through the seat to the horse's back. (021).

– Unilateral aids (rein and leg on the same side) act as containing aids. (See section 031, framing the horse)
– Diagonal aids (example: Inside leg and outside rein[1]), influence the horse in active and passive diagonal pairs. They are used to straighten the horse; or to form the horse on bent lines; or to establish the two-track positions.

INSIDE LEG: gives the active driving aid; the horse is bent around it.

ACTIVE PAIR:[2]

OUTSIDE REIN: controls the pace or rhythm; also controls the amount of bend. It is the chief guiding rein. (051, the half-halt).

The active aid is constituted by a nudging or vibrating within the application of pressure.

[1] How do we know which is the inside? This is determined by the rider. Regardless of on which hand one rides in the school, the direction in which the rider wishes to bend his horse will be the inside.

[2] The requirement of only one active aid at any one time still applies. **These tools are only to be active when necessary.** Once the desired reaction has been achieved from the horse, these active tools should INSTANTLY return to their home base of neutrality.

| | OUTSIDE LEG[3]: | holds the quarters from swinging out; as a driving leg, has the same pressure as inside leg but is held passive 022. |
| PASSIVE PAIR: | | |

| | INSIDE REIN: | asks for the bend (that's all!) (017g, 027). |

The passive aid is comprised in the application of a steady, uniform pressure.

WHAT FUNCTION DOES THE HAND PLAY?

IN its function as regulator of the pace, the hand can be compared to the nozzle on the end of a garden hose. When the rider does not take up the contact (loose rein), it would be the same as completely removing the nozzle from the hose; the water, not being restricted, just falls out. When the contact is taken up, the nozzle now starts to play the role of accurately controlling the amount of water leaving the hose. When the nozzle is shut, the water (horse) stops. When the nozzle opens more or less, and depending upon the amount of pressure generated by the pump (driving aids), the result is either a fine, powerful mist (collected work, Piaffe), or a strong, forceful jet of water (extended trot).

If there is no pressure control on the pump (ruthless, insensitive use of driving aids), and should the nozzle be shut (hard, resisting hand), the hose would rupture somewhere along its length (the horse first becomes excited, then if pressure isn't released, the horse would 'explode' by either rearing, or bucking-out behind to relieve the overload of pressure in its body. The more mild manifestations of this would be: tensions, stiffness, resistance, rushing, constrained motion, choppy gaits).

The nozzle is only of value as a PASSIVE control when the water

[3] When the leg is in the normal position (011, a) it acts on the horse as a driving aid. If the leg is held back from this position by 4"-5", it acts as a containing aid when passive, and a sideways-yielding aid when active.

40

pump operates properly. Similarly, the hand only functions correctly when the driving aids supply it with sufficient forward energy.

THE VOICE: Horses react quite readily to the voice. This can be used advantageously especially during training. When sounds are calm and soothing, they have a relaxing, confiding effect. If, however, the voice is stern or sharp it can be used as a mild form of punishment.

SPURS AND RIDING
CROPS: These are considered artificial aids, and are only implemented to sharpen the response to the natural aids. 024, 060.

019
THE CORRECT ATTITUDE AND DRIVING INFLUENCE
FROM THE SEAT (see illustrations on page 59)

IT cannot be sufficiently strongly emphasized, that the rider learns to command a good position and master a precise control over his lower back, in order to be able to concentrate his weight correctly into the seat bones.

In 'stilling' the back while keeping the seat well tucked-under (bracing the back), the rider directly influences the presence of the hindquarter, and the horse's centre of balance beneath his seat, enabling him to hold the horse in front of him. The 'essence' of the driving seat is constituted in a sitting more deeply into the motion of the horse. It is principally a weight aid which can be given with greater or lesser intensity.

THE OPTIMUM THE SEAT CAN DO IS TO BE
ABSOLUTELY QUIET IN RELATIONSHIP TO THE HORSE.

– Points of the optimum driving influence from the seat:–

   1) Head held upright.

41

2) A truly VERTICAL, QUIET and stretched upper body. (well drawn-back shoulders).
3) A flat, supple back (not hollowed or rounded).
4) Seat bones held quietly and elastically into the front of the saddle.

With this attitude the rider INCREASES his weight in the seat, the centre of balance falling toward the back of the seat bones. The optimum driving influence comes from the combined use of the seat with coinciding pressure from both legs.

– Points of the complete NON-DRIVING attitude from the seat:–

1) Upper body leaning forward and/or
2) Completely limp, relaxed lower back and/or
3) Lower back hollowed.
4) The forward seat (jumping), the rider's seat is taken completely out of the saddle.

With this attitude the seat is made LIGHTER; the rider's centre of balance falls in front of the seat bones.

020
INCORRECT ATTITUDES AND DRIVING INFLUENCE OF THE SEAT AND POSITION

– Head nodding, looking down
– Shoulders heaving, rounded
– Back hunched; upper body leaning forward or backward
– Much pelvic movement; sloppy loose back; stomach flopping (especially at sitting trot)
– Unquiet knees; thighs rolling
– Sitting on crotch, thighs or seat muscles
– Exaggerated tapping with lower legs; heels drawn up
– Any rigidity or stiffness, tensions. These result in the seat bouncing in the saddle, and unquiet hands that flap up and down at each trot or canter stride
– It is incorrect to think of the driving from the seat to be an active pushing motion on the saddle.

021
WHAT IS A WEIGHT AID?

THE weight aid is constituted in the rider's ability to determine precisely where his weight (centre of balance) falls into his seat bones. Firstly, when the weight falls toward the front or back of the seat bones (bilateral weight aid), it influences the horse as a driving aid (019). Secondly, by increasing the weight in one or the other seat bone (unilateral weight aid), it influences the horse as a bending or steering aid (027, 1).

The weight aids only become truly effective once the rider is able to sit quietly, and cause his centre of balance to coincide with the horse's centre of balance (putting the horse correctly on the aids 036, 037).

022
THE TIMING OF THE DRIVING AID FROM THE LEGS

THE horse can only be asked for an increase in stepping or activity when its hind leg is about to come off the ground (moment of thrusting-off) and during the time when it is in the air. The horse cannot react to activating aids when the hind foot is on the ground. (During the weight-bearing phase).

At the walk:–	BOTH legs of the rider activate the corresponding hind foot of the horse ACTIVELY. (An alternating left-right aid).
At the trot and canter:–	The rider's inside leg gives the aid actively; the outside leg giving the same pressure but remaining passive.*

---

* Both legs may be used actively to drive, when a strong aid is necessary – it should, however, be the exception. Always remember to consider the appropriate driving attitude from the seat while activating.

IMPORTANT FACTORS ABOUT ACTIVATING THE HORSE

IN the ability to activate, lies one of the most important fundamental requirements of the riding task. Only when the rider can initiate and control the true forward urge, and allows it to occur, will he actually control the horse correctly. When the horse goes truly forward, a multitude of evasions and problems are automatically eradicated 043.

1. Never drive the horse more than it accepts or tensions will be caused in it's back.
2. As is commonly known, true work doesn't begin until the horse becomes lazy. The horse must let itself be driven. The rider must not mistake nervous or excited energy for true forward impulse. The horse must first be relaxed and in the correct rhythm before it can be asked for more stepping from behind.
3. If the rider forces his horse forward, despite the animal's hard, hollow back, he will only cause the horse to resist further, and find evasions in crookedness, rushing, or a constrained forward motion.
4. The activating aids should not degenerate into a physical moving of the horse. It should be an effortless task to send the horse on. This can be achieved only when the rider has a clear mental intention while activating: Think of attaining a LONGER stride and/or a ROUNDER motion while remaining in the same rhythm 051. Remember to ALLOW the horse to go forward through the light hands.

TUNING THE HORSE TO AIDS FROM THE SEAT AND LEGS

IF a horse should become dull, one can sharpen the response as follows:–

1. The correct aid from the seat and legs has been given . . . the horse responds sluggishly.
2. Repeat the aid from seat and leg, and simultaneously enforce the aid with use of the stick or spurs (the stick for supporting the forward aid; the spurs for supporting the sideways-yielding aids).*
3. Upon which immediately renew the aid with the legs and seat alone.
4. This sequence is to be repeated until the horse responds willingly, without the support of the artificial aids.

025

THE QUALITY OF THE REIN CONTACT

(a)   Soft and light.
(b)   Elastic at all times.
(c)   Even though the contact needs to become heavier for short moments (when offering the horse resistance), it may never become HARD.

The rein aids must be transmitted through a continuous contact; never from a flapping, slack 'wash line'.

The softness, elasticity and sensitivity of the contact originates from an entirely independent upper body and is transmitted through supple, relaxed shoulders, elbows and wrists to warm friendly fists. (Such as a pleasant hand shake between people.)

The limp, opened little hand, that holds the reins towards the fingertips, is to be avoided.

026

QUALITY, QUANTITY AND INTONATION OF THE AIDS

ANYONE can sit on a horse . . . pull on the reins . . . squeeze with the legs . . . or hit the horse with a crop. This in itself, however, obviously doesn't make one a good or effective rider.

The main task in all the years of learning how to administer correct

* This refers to the ideal use of the stick or spurs, their use can be interchanged when necessary.

45

aids is encompassed in the discovering of 'how much'. Not only must one measure-out exactly the correct amount, but the quality and texture of each aid also play an important, decisive role.

The horses have the uncanny talent for perceiving the most subtle nuances that are often transmitted subconsciously by the rider. If, therefore, the horseman learns to channel these mental intentions positively, it facilitates a completely new horizon of communication with the animal.

In the telling of jokes lies an example of the intonation which can colour the aids. The words alone, however clever they might be, play only a relatively small part in the presentation of wit. When the feeling for suitable expression, gesture and timing is lacking, the joke often falls flat. Similarly within the giving of aids, one can either fail or succeed, depending frequently only upon this appropriate inflection.

027

SEQUENCE OF CHANGING POSITION AND AIDS WHEN CHANGING THE REIN

THOUGH the position change is a rapid sequence, one must follow this order. (These points apply any time the horse is being bent)

1) CHANGE THE SEAT   The inside seat bone must be slightly ahead of the outside one, and with a bit more weight in it.

2) CHANGE THE DRIVING LEG   The horse must be bent around the inside leg which acts like a post. It also gives the active driving aid. Always make a clear distinction in changing the leg position: inside leg in the normal position (O11, a), the outside leg held well back (4"-5") supporting the quarters from swinging-out.

3) CHANGE THE BENDING REIN AIDS   These will only be obeyed when the seat and leg aids have been correct. The bending rein aids should always be given in an elastic, ASKING manner.

REFLECTIONS III

- Only a truly suppled, relaxed horse can correctly obey a rein aid.
- Our reactions must be lightning-quick; but our attitude towards the horse should be as though we had all the time in the world.
- Always prepare yourself mentally and physically before asking your horse for anything.
- It must be the rider's chief aim to cause the horse to respond to ever lighter aids.
- In putting the horse on the aids it is imperative that we have the horse well 'on' the inside leg and outside rein.
- It must be considered a serious fault to ride the horse with the crop or spurs only, without first having given the aid properly with seat and legs.
- When driving from the seat; the holding of the seatbones into the front of the saddle (tucking the seat under), should not result in the tensing of the rider's stomach muscles.
- Never ambush (surprise) your horse with any aid.
- The side of that rein and leg of the rider, reacts directly on the corresponding hind foot of the horse.
- The energy which is generated by the leg in POUNDS . . . should be received within the hand in OUNCES.
- No aids will more adversely affect the horse than harsh, unfeeling rein aids.
- Only once the rider becomes quiet, will the horse be able to hear the whispers of the finer aids.
- The hands must give the hind legs space to step, they should have a yielding attitude toward the horse's mouth.
  When, due to activity, the horse shortens its frame, it is perfectly acceptable to FOLLOW the horse's head back with the hands (to avoid losing the contact), . . . as opposed to actively pulling backward, in an attempt to force the head into place.
- We must have a clear mental intention while giving any aid, or the riding will degenerate quickly into strictly a physical task.

Barty. 'Forward and down' at the working trot (see 038).

CHAPTER IV

THE HORSE

028

THE PRINCIPLES OF RIDING

THE three cardinal principles of riding are: Forward, Calm and Straight.

1. FORWARD – Horse going actively in correct rhythm. An unconstrained, fluid motion, neither rushing nor lazy.

   – Rushing means, the horse is going in too fast a rhythm. (chasing, unbalanced, on forehand).

   – Lazy means, that the horse may well be in the correct rhythm, but isn't active from behind.

2. CALM – The horse is calm when it is psychologically at ease; in a cooperative, unagitated state of mind.

   – The horse is not calm when:–
      (a) Adversely affected by outside stimuli (includes the rider).
      (b) High from being in the stall for a long time. Over-feeding of grain combined with insufficient work.
      (c) When it is nervous.

3. STRAIGHT –   A horse is straight when its hind feet travel in the same path the front feet take.

- Within the above requirement, the horse must also have its spinal column and neck bent exactly on the form of the line being ridden.
- The horse can be (and must be) straight, even while riding on a circle, or bent lines. The volte is the smallest curved line the horse can bend its whole body on (six meters). If the rider wishes to make smaller turns, then correct two-track work must be implemented, culminating in turns on the haunches.
- 'Straight' work is referred to as: WORK ON A SINGLE TRACK

029

THE SIX MAJOR GUIDELINES FOR CORRECT RIDING AND TRAINING

- Rhythm
- Suppleness
- Contact
- Straightened
- Impulsion
- Collection

It must be noted that these are individual stages of riding or training. One must have each single requirement before the next step can be attained. There must be an even correct rhythm before suppleness will be reached; only a supple horse will manifest a correct contact (which the horse searches for and takes up); after which straightening can be easily attained; only then can the rider ask for more impulsion, which after the appropriate length of training can be furthered to a true collection.

50

FUNDAMENTAL AIMS IN TRAINING THE HORSE

- Initial handling and longeing sessions to acquaint the youngster with the bridle, saddle and tack; and the first simple
  obedience lessons.
- The horse must become accustomed to the carrying and
  balancing of weight on a supple, elastic back.
- The horse must learn to obey the rider's wishes – control,
  responsiveness, accuracy in riding of school figures and
  execution of exercises.
- Gymnastic training; the building of muscle structure, tendons, heart and lungs for strength and endurance and fully
  developing the athletic qualities of balance and agility.
- Gradually and systematically, the more advanced exercises
  are introduced as the horse becomes able to cope with the
  work, without causing either physical or psychological damage.

When the horse is carefully steeped in a consistent routine; hand-
led with firm kindness and respect, the animal becomes mentally
mature and mellowed . . . a willing and generous worker, confident
in mankind 004 1–18.

031

FRAMING THE HORSE

- In order to gain precise control, the rider must 'frame' the horse.
- To frame means to CONTAIN the horse within the clear perime-
  ter of the rider's natural tools: the legs, hands, and seat. (018).
- The rider's legs and reins must form a channel (like two sheets of
  plywood), through which the horse is allowed forward. The left
  rein and leg contain the left side; the right rein and leg contain the
  right side.
- Both legs and both reins must have a continuous contact with the
  horse.

If the contact of any one of these is lacking, it gives the horse a hole
through which it can escape, crookedness may result and also a poor
control over the rhythm, activity and balance. It is particularly

essential that both reins stabilize the neck onto the withers, quietly and passively preventing any snakiness of the neck at this location.

Even if the rider has a contact with both reins and legs there are more subtle ways in which the animal is not framed. These are some of the common evasions:–

(a) Opening or crossing the jaw. (Can be prevented by appropriate adjustment of the noseband; riding with a light hand.)

(b) The drawing-up or sticking-out of the tongue. (The result of riding with hard, dominating, or dead hands.)

(c) The horse's neck is bent (laterally) more than the curve of the line being ridden. (Prevails when the horse is not bent evenly throughout its body. The neck is over-bent being broken sideways just ahead of the withers). The horse can escape the rider by falling against the outside shoulder, or running-out. (Can be prevented by straightening the horse, and using the outside rein and leg more clearly as a wall.)

(d) The horse breaking its neck (horizontally) at the third vertebra behind the poll. The neck and spinal column are no longer a continuous entity. The horse escapes the rider by making its neck too short and thereby coming behind the bit. This is a result of forced riding, the horse's head has been pulled down without regard for the natural balance. (Can be corrected by strong forward riding [maintain the rhythm] and forward and downward exercises. 038.)

(e) The horse tipping its head sideways (warping of the neck). Can be a result of forced riding; or lack of forward urge; or riding with a predominating hand; the horse is bottled-up; unequal pressure in reins.

032
THE FRAMING ACTION OF THE SEAT

BY sitting down correctly, the rider holds his horse IN FRONT of him. This directly influences the PRESENCE of the hind quarters underneath the seat and prevents the horse from going in a broken-apart manner: HE WHO HAS CONTROL OF THE HIND FOOT OF HIS HORSE, CONTROLS THE WHOLE HORSE. (008, 019)

033

CRITERION FOR CORRECT HEAD POSITION OF THE HORSE

1. Poll is the highest point of the whole horse.
2. Nose slightly ahead of, or on the vertical line.
3. Ears on the same level. (head not tipping sideways).

034

COMPLETION OF THE CIRCUIT

THE circuit can only be complete if both horse and rider are entirely void of tensions and resistance. Only through suppleness can the horse's hindquarter react correctly to the driving aids and start to carry more weight. (043)

The rider, being the motivator of the action, causes his horse to step actively through its back. The impulse travels through the horse's spinal column, the neck, poll and jaw to the bit, through the reins into the riders' fists, elbows shoulders and the rider's back, which reacts directly, once again, upon the horse's back. This completion of circuit (leg in hand) is the basis for all work.

035

'ON THE AIDS' – VERSES – 'COLLECTION'

IT is generally believed that if the horse's head has been brought down (regardless of how this has been attained), the horse is therefore 'collected'. This is not in keeping with riding in accordance with classical principles.

A horse must be 'put on the aids', which RESULTS in the correct head position, in order to show ANY correct work. A horse which is 'on the aids' is thereby prepared to execute the three gaits from EXTREME EXTENSIONS to the highest degree of collection (depending on its individual level of training).

Collection in itself, however, is a state attained only after many years of systematic, gymnastic work, and manifests itself in a shorter, higher stride, not lacking in fluidity or forward impulse, nor showing loss of the correct sequence of footfall in the gaits. True collection is marked by a clear lowering of the croup, because of bent haunches that carry more weight.

Reference is made in the photo captions to "SHORTENED" working gaits. This term is used to signify the shortening of the stride at a stage of training in which the horses are not yet sufficiently advanced to demonstrate the true 'collected' or 'School gaits'. The shortened gaits should be clearly active; the elements which are lacking are the lowering of the croup and the elevated motion of the legs, which is only found in true collection.

036
WHAT DOES 'ON THE AIDS' MEAN?

THE horse which is being ridden on the loose rein is like a bow which has not yet been strung, one cannot quickly or effectively shoot arrows with it. When the horse is put 'on the aids', its body becomes spanned like a compressed spring . . . the strung bow. This compression occurs when the horse obeys the activating aids and commences to step impulsively through its back; the hindquarter becomes more loaded, the centre of balance moves backward beneath the rider's seat; because of the forward impulse, the horse's neck rises UP off the withers and upon finding resistance at the bit, it yields at the poll resulting in the correct head position 033. When this state can be maintained in the three gaits through all simple school figures and upward or downward transitions, then the horse is considered to be well 'on the aids'.

It is particularly through the unity of centres of balance, which occurs when the horse is correctly put on the aids that the horse becomes liberated, allowing it uninhibited motion and enables it to respond easily and instantly to the rider's wishes. Only when this coinciding of centres of balance materializes, do the weight aids from seat and upper body find their true impact.

When the young horse is put on the aids, the neck rises very gently off the withers and the nose is still well in front of the vertical. With more advanced horses (which have improved in their balance, suppleness and activity) the neck rises more markedly up from the withers, and the nose comes closer to the vertical. The correct head position (033) is only of value when it is the END RESULT of the horse balancing itself by stepping actively through its back.

54

HOW IS THE HORSE PUT 'ON THE AIDS'?

IT is essential that the rider learns to put the horse 'on the aids' quickly and effectively. It is the fundamental state from which all work commences. To put the horse on the aids the rider must cause it to respond to the following series of aids:–

- the forward driving aids
- the bending aids
- the sideways-yielding aids from the legs.

- as a RESULT of response to the above three categories of aids, the animal will consequently begin to react to the restraining aids from the reins. (Remember, the reins play largely a passive, receiving role)

- The horse should be put on the aids at the walk (young horses excepted 044), by riding voltes and bent lines with frequent changes of rein. (See 055)
- The horse must be framed 031.
- The rider must offer the horse an even elastic contact 025.
- It is essential to maintain an absolutely even, correct rhythm to cause the horse to relax its back (the half-halt plays an important role 051).
- The rider must, as needed, continuously 'lure' impulsive forward stepping from the hindquarter, activating the horse into both reins.

Only through tactfulness and sensitivity can a favourable response be expected from the horse. In projecting his quietening influence, the rider gains the animal's confidence and contributes to the general relaxation.

In the appropriate ratio between the activating aids from seat and legs, and the suitable restraining aids from the hands, lies the key to control over the increased loading of the hindquarter, and therefore the balance of the horse. This balanced state must be born out of the forward impulse of the three gaits (referred to as RELATIVE ERECTION of head and neck); it can only be achieved and maintained through the predominating use of the driving aids.

If the horse's head has been brought down through the direct, positive use of the hand, the backward-working hand, (referred to as ACTIVE ERECTION of head and neck), the resulting exterior appearance of the horse will have no co-relation to either the impulsion, or the use of the horse's back. (The German Master, Julius Walzer, was known to have said "With the unknowledgeable rider the art starts at the horse's neck, and it also desists there. . .")[*]

038
FORWARD AND DOWN

THE forward and down exercise is not merely used as a transitionary stage in the training of young horses (to teach them to stretch for the bit). One should be able to demonstrate the forward and down with any horse, at any stage of the training. Forward and down is the sign that the horse has been correctly worked (from back to front), and that its back muscles are elastically in play, originating from a lively, impulsive hindquarter.

Once the horse has been put on the aids, the forward and down exercise can be asked for (it isn't necessary to put young horses 'on the aids' before practicing this exercise, any forward and downward stretching, in the early stages of training, should be allowed and encouraged). As the rider gradually lets the horse's head stretch towards the ground, care must be taken to keep the contact while maintaining the impulsion and a steady rhythm. The horse's nose must remain at (or in front of) the vertical. One can easily bring the horse's head back up to the correct position by increasing the impulsion but maintaining the rhythm.

With young horses, the forward and down is best executed with a light seat at the walk and canter, and only at the rising trot. With older horses the exercise can be done with a full seat in all three gaits. To complete this exercise, one should be well versed in putting the horse on the aids, and have a steady position and clear, consistent giving of aids.

[*] Meister der Reitkunst, Waldimar Seunig, Erich Hoffmann Verlag 1960; Page 80.

Barty. 'Forward and down' at the canter left.

039
EQUAL LOADING OF THE HORSE'S LEGS

BESIDES the equal loading of front and hind legs, which balances the horse and causes it to find the correct head position, the legs must also be equally loaded left and right.[1] If the horse is properly suppled and on the aids, this equal loading occurs naturally. (043)
– Indications of the horse NOT having equal weight on inside and outside legs: (from tensions and resistance)

- Horse leaning on one rein.
- Horse's body bulging against one of the rider's legs.
- Horse going crooked.
- Head tipping (ears not on same level).
- Unlevel gait.

1. Lateral equilibrium.

57

REFLECTIONS IV

- When training the horse – do little and frequently.
- Any artificial placement of the horse's head, must be strictly avoided.
- It is damaging to the horse's gaits, to ride ANY exercise in two-track work, turns on the haunches or gaits other than ORDI-NARY walk, trot or canter, unless the horse is first correctly put 'on the aids'.
- Correct lateral bending (left, right) is one of the keys to horizontal bending, or yielding, in the horse's back, and therefore the poll. (037) (043)
- It must be repeatedly impressed upon each rider, to instill in his horse the urge to move forward fluidly.
- LET-THROUGH-ABLE! That state in which the horse allows the energy from the hindquarter through its whole body. (034 complete circuit).
- One will always be able to trace any riding problem to the breaking of one, or all, of the cardinal rules of horsemanship; 'forward, calm and straight'. (028)
- If the horse is trained by force; force will be required to ride it.
- If the horse should become over-bent (nose behind the vertical) the driving aids must be used to raise the head to the correct position. Never use the hand with sharp upward jerks.
- It is essential that the moment the horse yields to the rein pressure, the rider also instantly yields and becomes light with his hand. (016 d)
- The most difficult task the horseman has to perform is to ride, purely and accurately, the three basic gaits: walk, trot and canter 'on the aids'. Once this has been TRULY mastered, the advanced exercises are relatively easy, being a logical result of CORRECT basic work.

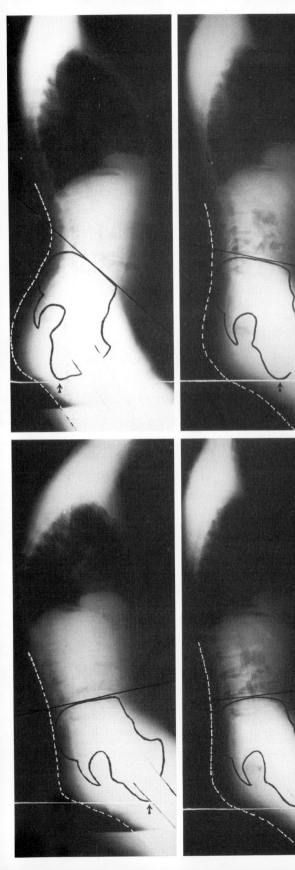

On this page is a series of actual X-rays of the Author's position, which clarify the various attitudes of the pelvis and back. The horizontal white line represents the flat surface upon which the seat bones rest. The pelvis is outlined in black. The arrow locates the weight-bearing point of the seat bones. The thigh bone is lightly outlined. The broken white line marks the flesh extremities of the back. The transverse black line shows the tilt of the pelvis. (See 019).

Top left
Hollow back. This common fault is also often seen with the upper body leaning forward or backward.

Top right
Correct normal seat.

Bottom left
Hunched back. This incorrect attitude is frequently misconstrued as a bracing. The upper body is completely collapsed, the weight is dissipated and cannot be effectively concentrated into the seat bones.

Bottom right
Braced back. The driving ATTITUDE of the correct seat.

59

Atlantis. Turn on the haunches, right.

CHAPTER V

THE EXERCISES; THE THREE GAITS; TWO TRACK WORK THE SCHOOL FIGURES

040
CATEGORIES OF EXERCISES

1. Loosening (042) Exercises (Preparatory Exercises)	–	walk on the loose rein
	–	rising trot
	–	turns on the forehand
	–	leg-yielding
	–	asking the horse to bend right and left at the standstill
	–	with some horses an easy canter for a few minutes (light seat)
	–	frequent transitions from trot to canter and back to trot.
	–	'forward and down' riding (038)
2. Suppling (043) Exercises (Actual work starts here)	–	riding voltes, serpentines and circles.
	–	frequent changes of rein
	–	riding positions right and left alternately on the long sides (walk, trot)
	–	lengthening and shortening the stride in three gaits
	–	frequent riding of transitions
	–	halt and rein-back
	–	shoulder-in

3. Collecting		
Exercises	–	shoulder-in
	–	renverse (no longer a required exercise)
	–	traverse
	–	turns on the haunches
	–	halt and rein-back
	–	counter-canter
	–	all suppling exercises can be included

4. Collected Work.	–	three collected gaits
(The High School	–	canter pirouettes
of dressage)	–	flying changes
	–	piaffe and passage

5. The airs above the ground.

041

THE IMPORTANCE OF RIDING ON 'STRAIGHT LINES'

BENDING exercises are used to supple, in order to be able to straighten the horse! It is essential that plenty of work on STRAIGHT LINES also be ridden; on the second track, across diagonals and centre line (away from the school walls).

While riding on straight lines, the rider must sit exactly squarely in the saddle, with both legs in the SAME position (the outside leg is NOT held back).

042

ELABORATION ON THE LOOSENING EXERCISES (040 1)

THE loosening exercises aid the rider to initially eradicate stiffness from the horse. During these exercises, simple, large school figures should be utilized, and sharp turns avoided.

It is a sound practice to begin each session with a few minutes of 'walk on the loose rein'. It inspires confidence and relaxation within the horse, and serves the rider as a moment to settle down, while preparing mentally for the work to come.

The turning of the horse's head slightly right and left at the stand-still serves – (a) to further the suppleness of the poll and jaw. (b) to teach both horse and rider, that the inside rein is only used to bend the horse. It is not to be used to pull the horse about (like a coach horse).

Leg-yielding and turns on the forehand must be practiced sparingly; they DISENGAGE the hindquarter. These exercises can be used in the early training of the horse, to teach responsiveness to leg pressure. Furthermore, it is beneficial to the learner rider, in discovering how to co-ordinate the aids.

Important points:–	–	Only a very slight bend to the inside.
(leg-yielding and	–	Inside leg and outside rein dominate.
turns on forehand)	–	Horse no more than 45 degree angle to the wall. (While leg-yielding).
Common mistakes are	–	Pulling the horse around with the inside rein.
	–	Letting the horse rush around, without clearly stopping after each step. (During turns on forehand)
	–	Rider collapsing on the inside hip. (Not sitting squarely on both seat-bones)

Note. With well trained horses, after the initial walk on the loose rein, the loosening exercises are only started once the horse is put on the aids at the walk.

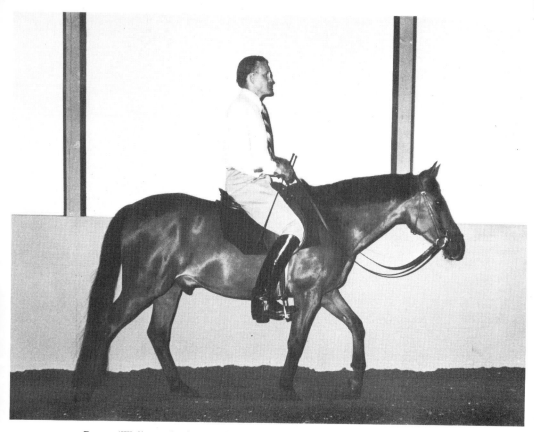

Barty. 'Walk on the loose rein' before any work has been done.

043

ELABORATION ON THE SUPPLING EXERCISES

THE suppling exercises are used to establish the horse more solidly on the aids; initiating the elasticity in the horse's back; gaining control over the hindquarter, and therefore the balance; and furthering the unity between horse and rider.

Any work on curved lines, with frequent changes of rein and riding of transitions, is beneficial to suppling the horse. The shoulder-in exercise is particularly helpful to aid the rider in softening the horse's stiff side.

The practical value of all exercises is only realized, if each individual rider, through methodical experimentation, discovers to which combination of loosening and suppling exercises his OWN horse responds most favourably. The immediate goal being, that the

64

horse puts its body entirely at the rider's disposal, without resistance or reservation, in as short a time as possible . . . THE BLANK CHEQUE STATE.

The practical aims in suppling the horse are:–

That the horse. . . . (a) moves freely forward.
(b) works equally well on both hands.
(c) does not lean on one rein. Willingly bends to either side from rein aids, properly supported with leg aids.
(d) readily yields to leg pressure, does not lean on, or bulge against, one of the rider's legs.

The feeling of working a horse correctly, is described in section 057.

044
WORK AT THE WALK

Definition:– (a) The walk has STEPS
(b) Four beat motion
(c) No moment of suspension.
Sequence:– 1. Right hind 2. Right front
3. Left hind 4. Left front.

The sequence of steps at the walk must comprise a distinct and DELIBERATE four beats, with an even, unhesitating rhythm. The walk is the least-impulsive gait, and is the most difficult in which to keep a strong forward urge.

This gait can, however, be advantageously used by the beginner rider, in learning how to administer his aids without being unnecessarily tossed about. It is also beneficial to practice any new exercises at the walk with young horses, before the work is requested in the higher gaits.

It must be strictly observed to ride the young horse at the walk on the long (or loose) rein only, until the second year of training. The youngster must first be well balanced and on the aids at the trot, before it can be put on the aids at the walk. The quality of the gaits can be permanently ruined if the horse is prematurely put on the aids at the walk. (Pace-walking can be one of the undesirable consequences.)

Modes of the walk:– Extended– Hind foot steps well beyond front print.

Ordinary– Hind foot steps into or just beyond front print.

Collected– Hind foot steps well behind front print. A higher, shorter motion.

045

VALUE OF 'WALK ON THE LOOSE REIN' WITHIN A WORKING SESSION

BESIDES the obvious value as a moment of rest for both horse and rider, the walk on the loose rein serves to RE-NATURALIZE the horse which may have become uncomfortable or resisting. It is also a helpful solution to those moments when one's blood boils due to frustrations, the walk on the loose rein can give the rider a clean slate, after a period of cooling off. After walking on the loose rein for a few minutes, one should take note of the smoother motion and the longer, easier stepping. When taking up the contact once again, care should be taken to preserve this fluidity.

While letting the reins out through the fingers, always DRIVE the horse into lengthening its neck forward and downward. The horse should gradually lengthen itself, as opposed to crassly jerking the reins from the rider's hands. When riding on the loose rein, the horse should not be allowed to 'slop' along lazily; it must be kept moving smartly and freely forward, through the continued presence of appropriate driving influence from the seat on the horse's back.

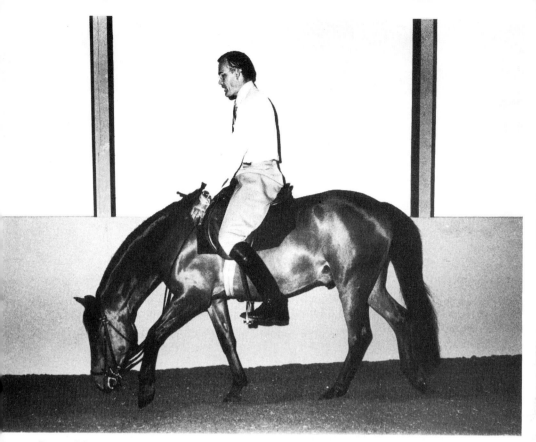

Barty. After some loosening exercises the horse drapes itself from relaxation. The horse stretches itself readily as the rider yields with the hands while driving. This attitude should be assumed any time 'Walk on the loose rein' is ridden within a working session. Compare with Plate on page 64.

046
WORK AT THE TROT

Definition:–		
	(a)	The trot has STRIDES
	(b)	Two-beat motion
	(c)	Moment of suspension after each stride.
	(d)	The presence of DIAGONAL UNISON is absolutely necessary. This means that within the motion of any diagonal pair of legs, both legs

Sequence:—

must leave the ground (or alight on the ground) at exactly the same moment. If the diagonal legs are not unified, an incorrect 3- or 4-beat motion results. See plates on page 101. Diagonal pairs of legs move alternately. There is a moment of suspension after each stride.

The bulk of the riding should be practiced at the trot. It is the shooling gait for both horse and rider. The work at both the walk and canter will only progress favourably once the trot work becomes mature. The trot is more impulsive than the walk. It is the best gait to use in teaching the horse to balance itself, first on the longe, later under the rider; learning to respond to the activating aids, becoming supple and using its back and hindquarter.

The rider's seat and position will only develop correctly after much work at the sitting trot (without stirrups). Once the rider has developed a good seat at the trot, then sitting well to the walk or canter poses few problems.

Modes of the trot:— Extended — Hind foot can step as much as 36″ beyond front print.

Middle — An energetic long trot, showing much knee and hock action. Hind foot steps well beyond front print.

Ordinary — (working trot) Hind foot steps into or just beyond the front print.

Collected — Hind foot steps far short of the front print. Croup lowered; a higher, rounder motion.

WORK AT THE CANTER

Definition:–   (a) The canter has JUMPS.

(b) Three-beat motion.

(c) A moment of suspension after the third beat.

(d) The horse is on the correct lead when the inside front leg is leading (unless counter canter is asked for).

Sequence:–   1) Outside hind foot.

2) A diagonal pair of legs (inside hindfoot, outside front foot).

3) Inside front foot; then the moment of suspension.

By its very nature (a series of jumps), the canter is the most impulsive gait. Nonetheless, special care must be focused on maintaining the true forward urge. It is a common mistake, to slow the rhythm down, or worse yet attempting to 'collect' the gait, through the active use of the reins only (the backward-working hand). The horse invariably falls on the forehand, and due to a combination of inactivity and tensions, the gait breaks apart; the diagonal pair of legs (second phase) no longer move simultaneously and an incorrect 4-beat motion results.

COUNTER CANTER. At the counter canter the horse leads with its OUTSIDE front leg. (eg. Horse leads with right front leg while on the left rein). The horse must always be bent in the direction of the leading leg. Counter canter is both a collecting exercise, and a preparatory exercise for the flying changes of lead.

DISUNITED OR CROSS-CANTER. This occurs when the horse switches its lead behind (or in front) only. The forehand leads right and the hindquarter leads left, or vice versa. This usually happens because the rider's outside leg is not clearly back (supporting the quarters), or because of imbalance of the horse, or tensions in its back.

Note: During any canter work the rider must keep the horse truly straight. Most horses tend to evade the honest loading of the inside hind foot by bringing the hindquarter toward the inside, it is a very common mistake.

Modes of the canter:-	Extended –	Horse gains much ground at each stride, must still be a 3-beat motion.
	Middle –	A strong impulsive canter not fully extended.
	Ordinary –	(working canter) Bulk of canter work should be executed at this pace. The length of stride between middle and collected canter.
	Collected –	The jumps are shorter and higher; not much ground is gained, the croup is well lowered and engaged. It must be fluid, not tense or choppy.

048

THE CANTER AID

THE horse must be well prepared, and responsive especially to the bending aids (supple).

(a)   Horse clearly bent around inside leg.

(b)   Inside leg in normal position (011, a); outside leg well back (027).

(c)   Inside seatbone slightly forward, with a bit more weight in it.

(d)   Let the horse through the light hands as the seat and inside leg say, "Canter-on!" The outside leg gives the same pressure but is held passive. A half-halt is given just before the aid to canter.

(e)   To maintain the canter, the aid to canter-on is repeated at each stride (to a greater or lesser degree).

70

Be cautious not to force or surprise the horse with the canter aid, as tensions and rushing will result. With young horses it is best to strike-off to the canter from the trot, using the corner of the school to help juggle-up the correct lead. One may need to reinforce the leg aid with the crop (either at the horse's inside shoulder, or behind the rider's outside leg), until the horse becomes familiar with the signal from seat (weight aid) and leg. One should not strike-off to the canter from the walk until well into the second year of training; the horse should first be well established in walk on the aids.

It is a common mistake to force the horse back into the canter immediately after the horse has fallen from the canter into an unbalanced, rushing trot. The rider should, in such instances, always take the time to bring the horse back to a good rhythmic, relaxed trot before striking-off at the canter once again. With more advanced horses one should make the transition down to the walk before commencing with the canter; improves the use of the horse's back, and engagement of the hindquarter.

049
TRANSITIONS

ALL transitions, upward or downward including halts and half-halts within any gait, are an occasion in which the rider must further activate his horse. Transitions must be decisive, fluid and forward in nature.

By and large, a transition or respective resulting gait will only be as good as the work in the previous gait.

050
THE HALT

AN experienced rider on a well-suppled horse can demonstrate halts, half-halts and reinback with feather-light contact. In a correct halt the horse should come to stand squarely and quietly on all four legs.

A truly correct halt can only be executed on a horse which is relaxed, well on the aids and using its back (complete circuit 034). The rider must activate the horse into a restraining hand. The hand

Atlantis. The halt. The horse is held 'at the aids' with seat and legs, the hand remains passive.

must filter the forward energy in a soft, elastic way. IT IS STRICTLY AN ATTITUDE OF THE HAND AND DOES NOT CONSTITUTE A PULLING IN ANY SENSE OF THE WORD. The hand should also not become hard and fixed, thereby snubbing off the impulsion, making it impossible for the hind legs to step under (018).

When correctly executed, the halt (and reinback) can be an effective key to the increased loading of the hindquarter, and also sharpen the general obedience of the horse. While halting or performing a half-halt the rider must keep his head up and have a well-stretched position 005, 009, 014.

THE HALF-HALT

THE half-halt is performed in exactly the same way as the complete halt; to be correct and effective, the horse must respond to the forward driving aids. The only difference being: once the rider has driven the horse into the restraining hand, the hand yields just BEFORE the horse comes to the halt, allowing uninterrupted forward motion . . . as the legs and seat continue to ask for renewed activity. At the trot, the hand would yield just before the horse is about to walk; and at the canter, one would yield with the hand just before breaking into the trot.

This is an extremely exaggerated example of the half-halt, and the rider should learn to perform the half-halt in a much more subtle way, so that the observer cannot see the horse drastically changing its pace.

Half-halts give the rider the possibility to activate the horse (a more springy stepping) without changing the rhythm, while in motion. It also serves as an introductory signal to the horse, before corners, before changing the bend and before all transitions. It helps the rider maintain the horse's centre of balance beneath his seat, without the horse taking the hand (leaning).

The half-halt should never be a jerking on the outside rein; at most, it is a little squeeze WITHIN THE OUTSIDE FIST ITSELF, and can actually be executed without an active hand altogether, using the activating aid, and receiving the energy with a momentary resisting ATTITUDE in the hand.

It is highly undesireable to incessantly move the bit around in the horse's mouth – to 'saw the horse's head down' so to speak. Half-halts should only be used when necessary, not just for good measure.

- The rider's driving aids say, "A BIT MORE ACTIVITY".
- The hand says, "BUT STAY IN RHYTHM." (then yields)

DRIVE . . . RECEIVE . . . BECOME LIGHTER AGAIN.

THE REIN-BACK

THE rein-back originates from the activating aids. In this case, however, the seat is lightened by tipping the upper body SLIGHTLY forward. This allows the horse to go backward.

The rider's legs say, "Move" . . .

All the hands say is, "Not forward". The hand is strictly not to pull the horse backward.

To stop the rein-back, the rider merely sits upright again, presses his seat into the front of the saddle, while yielding with the hands.

The correct rein-back is constituted in a diagonal STEPPING (two-beat motion, without a moment of suspension). If the horse has a resisting back, or if the rider's hand actively pulls backward on the reins, an incorrect four-beat motion results. The horse's legs must be picked up clearly. The dragging feet are a sign of incorrect work, ie. resistance or tensions.

To use more than 5 – 6 steps of rein-back at any one time would constitute a punishment. Making any more than ten backward steps becomes unacceptable, because it endangers the tendons and joints which can suffer damage from this senseless practice.

Both the halt and rein-back must be executed with a straight horse; any lateral evasions must be carefully prevented.

Upper. Barty. Rein-back. Here the horse is still in an unfinished state of training, which is indicated by the relatively open position of the head. This originates from difficulties in the back (a non-yielding), and is also indicated by the unhappy expression on the horse's face.

Lower. Atlantis. Rein-back. Here a more advanced horse in exactly the same rein-back phase as the upper photo. Showing a good attitude psychologically, and a correct yielding attitude of the neck (back). The rider is just in the process of erecting the upperbody and bracing the back to come to the halt. Comparatively, the upper photo shows clearly the 'unloading' of the horse's back (rider leaning forward) during the actual process of reining-back. In both photographs a correct diagonal stepping is illustrated.

THE DEFINITION OF TWO-TRACK WORK

– The two-track exercises, which can be practiced in all three gaits are:–

  – Shoulder-in (054)
  – Travers
  – Renvers
  – Leg-yielding (walk and trot only. See 042)

Any work which is NOT ridden straight (i.e. on a single track, 028) is referred to as 'two-track' work, this is irrespective of whether the horse's legs make three or four separate tracks. The forehand and the hindquarter each travel on their own separate paths.

Correct two-track work should not be confounded with an uncontrolled crookedness, which the horse might offer as an evasion. It is not recommendable for a beginner rider to practice any two-track work (leg-yielding excepted), until he is very thoroughly acquainted with riding the horse 'on the aids' on all school figures, in the three basic gaits; riding these perfectly straight ON A SINGLE TRACK. (028)

It is beyond the scope of this brief text to engage in a detailed study of the values of two-track work. Basically, however, this work can either be implemented as an end in itself, or it can be used by experienced trainers to further the suppleness and activity of the back, hocks and hindquarter, improving the general malleability of the horse.

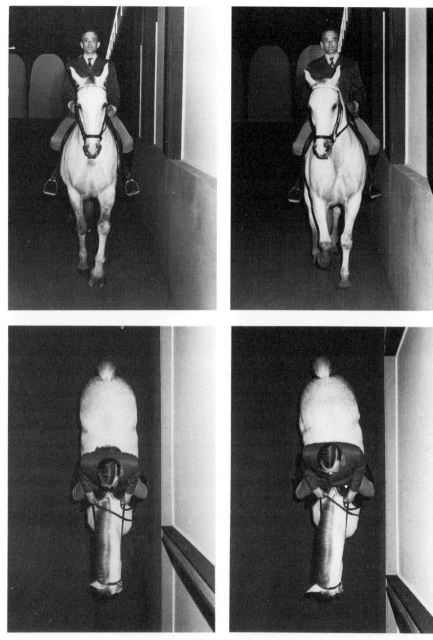

Work on the straight line (028, 041). From above, the rider's hips and shoulders are exactly square, sitting over the centre of the horse. When observing the horse from the front, one should see only TWO legs.

Position right. It should be noted that in all these photos, the horse travels parallel to the school walls.

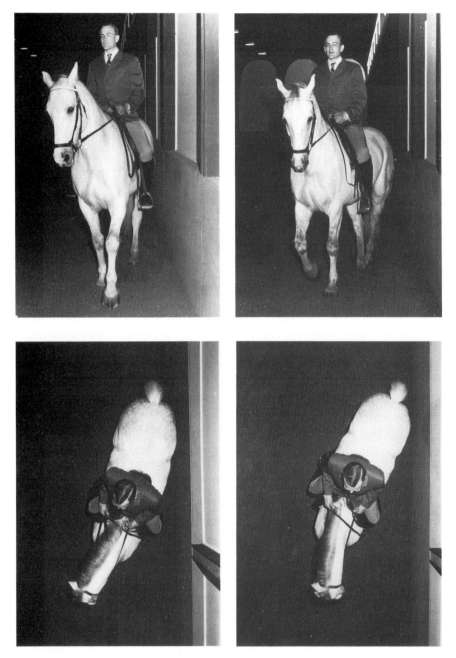

Shoulder-in right. This represents the
SECOND POSITION. (See foot note 054).

Renverse. (The reverse exercise to
traverse).

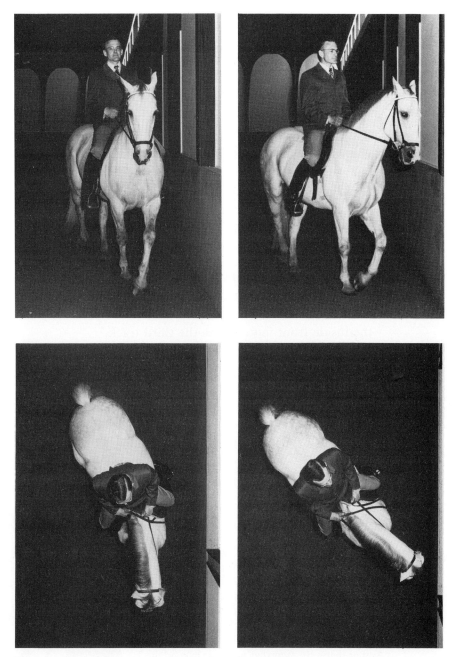

Traverse right. (When practised across the diagonal of the school it is called HALF-PASS).

Leg-yielding, away from left leg. Can also be practised with the horse facing toward the inside of the school 042.

SHOULDER-IN
OF WHAT VALUE IS THE SHOULDER-IN EXERCISE?

(a) Helps the rider supple the stiff side of his horse, and therefore contributes to the straightness.

(b) Helps to put the horse more clearly onto the inside leg and outside rein.

(c) Helps to further the suppleness and activity of the hindquarter. It can therefore be used as a collecting exercise.

(d) It is the basic preparatory exercise for all other two-track (lateral) work in all three gaits.

TECHNICAL REQUIREMENTS (description of the full shoulder-in or SECOND POSITION)[1]

(a) The exercise is ridden on three tracks. The outside hind foot makes one track; the inside hind foot follows exactly in the path of the outside front foot, making the second track; last, the inside front foot, makes the third track.[2]

(b) The horse must be bent through its whole body. The hindquarter travels straight along the wall. Only the forehand is brought slightly over to the inside of the school.

PRACTICAL IMPLEMENTATION (applies to all two-track work)

(a) The horse must be 'on the aids', before attempting the exercise.

(b) Care must be taken to remain sitting squarely in the saddle. Do not collapse onto the inside hip.

[1] THE FIRST POSITION is basically the same exercise as the SECOND POSITION but the horse does not come off the wall quite so far. In the FIRST POSITION the inside hind foot travels on a path which runs exactly between both front legs. It is also caled SOULDER-FORE, a preparatory exercise for the shoulder-in.

[2] Some classical masters have recommended the shoulder-in to be on 4 tracks, with the forehand yet further from the wall (both front and hind legs crossing). This Author shares the view that any angle beyond the 3 tracks would be a form of leg-yielding, which would therefore not be a collecting exercise 042.

(c) If problems arise (crookedness, resistance or constrained forward motion), the horse must be corrected by further straightening and suppling in SINGLE-TRACK WORK. 028.

(d) Shoulder-in, as with all two-track work, must be practiced with great discretion. The bulk of our work should be carried out on a single track. The horse's gaits (especially the forward urge) suffer adversely when two-track work is practiced superfluously.

Barty. Shoulder-in left. The outside hand is slightly raised to prevent the horse from falling over the outside shoulder. The rider's inside leg causes the inside hind foot to reach clearly under, which is the prime purpose of the exercise – ie., collection.

Barty. Half-pass right at the trot (traverse). Once the horse is properly suppled, the half-pass becomes fluid. Note the correct diagonal unison and the pronounced crossing of the hind legs. An impulsive 'forward-sideways' movement.

OF WHAT VALUE IS THE RIDING OF SCHOOL FIGURES?

THE school figures give the rider a purpose whereby he can assess his riding and evaluate where his control is lacking. Furthermore, when the figures are ridden 'forward – calm – straight' (028), they become a valuable tool in helping the learner rider to put his horse on the aids.

056

THE SCHOOL FIGURES

THE school figures should be practiced equally on both hands in order to exercise and develop the complete muscle structure and balance of the horse.

There are certain factors concerning the riding of the school figures which require some explanation. These points are not included in the diagrams:–

(a) It is important to ride well into the corners of the school. Here the rider can learn to bend the horse around his inside leg, and ask for activity without the horse rushing from the driving aids. Take note, however, that with unbalanced young horses the corners should be well rounded-off especially at the trot and canter.

(b) While riding on large circles, an excellent exercise to practice is to make the circle smaller by gradually spiralling towards the centre until it is VOLTE size, then enlarging it gradually to full size once again.

(c) The riding on the second track (6ft. to 8ft. from the school walls, riding parallel to the walls), is an ideal exercise to emphasize the need to frame the horse at all times (031). While practicing this exercise the rider should ride diligently into the IMAGINARY corners.

The following diagrams represent the fundamental school figures. See pages 108–111.

REFLECTIONS V

- Correct transitions are the proof of the pudding.
- Always bend the horse in the direction you are going. The only exceptions are: 1. Shoulder-in 2. Leg-yielding 3. Counter-canter.
- When riding any curved lines the horse must be bent throughout its body; not just the head and neck.
- In doing any two-track work remember to let the forehand ahead. The horse must move 'forward-sideways', rather than 'sideways-forward'.
- Simplicity is the strength of the exercise.
- When executing turns on the haunches, heed the following points:
    - (a) Keep the true forward intention.
    - (b) Do not pull the horse around with the inside rein.
    - (c) The correct sequence of walk steps must be maintained 044.
    - (d) Move off at the walk or trot immediately upon completion of the turn. (see PLATE 94)
- It is incorrect to press the horse toward the outside of a circle or turn, or ride through a corner, by bringing the inside rein against the neck. It is a sign that the inside leg is not doing its job, and the horse is also not 'on' the outside rein correctly.
- Only when we ourselves become truly ambidexterous, can we expect our horses to work equally well on both reins.
- Only bend your horse's neck until you see a glimpse of the inside eye and nostril rim (no more).
- The stability and balance within the horse can only be established through a resolute forward urge. This is fundamental in maintaining the purity of the gaits.*

---

* One must constantly regard the correct, even rhythm while activating, to prevent the problem of misconstruing a rushing or chasing with the honest and bold forward urge. 028, 023.

Barty. Working canter right.

CHAPTER VI

GENERAL OBSERVATIONS

THE fundamental task in the dressage riding lies in cultivating the ability to understand and speak "Horse", in the literal sense of the word.

The real problems begin the moment the rider wishes to influence the horse's way of going. So long as the rider 'hacks' his horse around inoffensively, he may not be improving on the basic motion of the gaits; however, he will also not produce the undesirable effects which result from implementing methods which are in conflict with the animal's nature.

While learning to influence the horse correctly, the rider can avoid complications by acquainting himself with the signals which are given by the horse, indicating its happiness or dissatisfaction with the work being asked of it. The next two sections outline these aspects in detail.

057
WHAT ARE THE SIGNS OF CORRECT WORK?

- The first sign that the horse is beginning to relax is that it starts to snort or 'blow'.
- The horse's back wells-up beneath the rider. The rib cage fills, making it easier to keep the legs on.
- The supple, swinging back becomes easy to sit on. The tail swings gently with the motion.
- The gaits become rounder; more clearly cadenced, springy.
- The horse is in front of the rider; the forehand becomes large and light (the shoulder is freed).
- The horse is easy to keep straight. Halts are easily executed and square. Transitions are fluid and clean.
- The good, soft, elastic feeling in the hand.

- The horse responds well to the driving aids. Its whole body readily lengthens, the gaits lengthen when the rider's hands yield towards the bit; in both extensions and collection the rhythm remains the same, not eratic.
- The horse's facial expression is quiet and accepting.
- As a result of stretching for the bit, relaxation and activity, the horse begins to chew QUIETLY, producing a FIRM foam on its lips. (When the saliva is too watery it is usually a sign of nervousness, characterized by a noisy, exaggerated biting at the bit.)

058

POINTS TO WATCH FOR IN INCORRECT WORK

PHENOMENON	REASON*
- stiffness, unwilling to bend.	- tensions[1] in back and neck, general resistance.
- rough trot and canter. (Hard to sit on).	- back not supple; circuit not complete; lack of activity, horse broken apart.
- too fast a rhythm, rushing.	- tension, discomfort, not relaxed in back; over-driving.
- grinding of teeth, noisy biting at the bit.	- horse unhappy; experiencing pain or rider forcing; lack of true forward; hard or dead hands.
- swishing of tail.	- rough aids; horse experiencing discomfort or pain, or is ticklish. (Caution with spurs!)

* If the horse should not appear to be 'performing as usual', the rider should keep in mind the possibility that the animal might not be feeling 100% well. It may be suffering from slight colic, cramps, stiffness, or might simply not be in 'good form', for what-ever physical or psychological reasons. The horse is not a machine!

[1] TENSIONS Tensions can be caused by a wide variety of reasons, usually, however, by the rider forcing the horse; or a method of training which has not come to grips with defences the horse uses against the rider, in order to avoid going to work; or the horse is not sufficiently prepared for the work being asked of it; or because of nervousness or fright. For an effective remedy see 028 through to 039.

- horse boring on the hand, (face often behind the vertical).
- lack of activity and therefore, balance; Horse rushing; on forehand.
- crookedness.
- horse not framed and/or not supple. Horse pressed together too soon into collected work. (Lameness)
- tossing of head.
- lack of balance and/or discomfort in back and/or rider's hands too unquiet and hard. Bridle badly adjusted. (Least likely, though possible, problems with teeth).
- forging or 'clicking' (Hind foot striking sole or shoe of front foot).
- horse on the forehand. Horse actively using hind legs, but the back is not in play (leggoer). (Possibly shoeing or trimming job not suited to horse's build and way of going).

059
WHICH BITS SHOULD BE USED?

MOST of the work in training of either horse or rider should be done with a plain, mild snaffle bit. Because the snaffle is broken in the middle it can act unilaterally on either side of the horse's mouth; a necessary prerequisite to teach the horse to yield to the bending aids. There is only one factor which determines the severity of the plain snaffle bit – the thinner the mouthpiece, the more severe the bit.

The double bridle is generally implemented as a formality in the showing of higher levels in dressage competitions. It is not necessarily a part of the horse's training; though it can, under certain circumstances, considerably alleviate the task in the ADVANCED training of particularly resistant, bullish horses. Use of the double bridle during such training should be temporary; the progress being frequently checked by testing the work on the snaffle. All Grand Prix exercises should be trained and ridden on a plain snaffle bit.

The curb bit has a single unbroken mouthpiece. Its shanks are a lever which, via the curb chain as a fulcrum, put pressure on both the tongue and bars in the mouth. The curb bit can only be used as a restraining or receiving tool; regulating the rhythm, and helping to maintain the balance within the horse. Therefore the bridoon is added in order to facilitate control over the bend as well.[1] There are four factors that determine the severity of the curb – the thinner the mouthpiece; the larger the port; the longer the shank; and last, the more tightly the curb chain is fitted – the more severe the curb bit.

Any bits, with the exception of the above mentioned, have no place in the riding in accordance with classical principles.

It cannot be sufficiently strongly advised never to punish the horse with the bit. This practice must be considered a gross brutality! It is highly destructive to the gaits, and annihilates the horse's confidence in the rider. If punishment is absolutely necessary, a more effective and less damaging alternative is to discipline the horse with a few smart whacks with the stick (004- 15).

060
THE USE OF AUXILIARY TACK

- Draw reins
- Chambon
- Side reins (other than for longeing)
- Martingales (standing or running)
- German running reins
- Very sharp spurs

All of these auxiliary aids, which are used to force the horse's head into place, HAVE NO USE IN THE NATURAL TRAINING OF THE HORSE.

---

[1] To ride on the curb only requires great experience, and the horse must be well prepared and supple as butter.

On very rare occasions (and then only in the most competent of hands), can side reins or draw reins be used on badly spoiled horses which continuously free themselves from the rider's aids because of severe tossing of the head; or to help stabilize horses with a particularly wobbly (spaghetti) neck; however, use should be discontinued as soon as possible (a temporary means to assist in eradicating specific problems).

Very sharp spurs are unhorsemanlike. The point at which an aid looses its effectiveness and becomes unacceptable, is when it starts to cause pain. (Where brutality begins, the art desists. E. von Neindorff). The spurs should be largely used to reinforce the sideways-yielding aids. The riding crop is a far more effective support for the driving aid because it directly initiates the natural desire to flee. The spurs, on the other hand, by and large, cause the horse to withold its fluid forward motion; they should be used sparingly and with discretion.

061

LONGEING THE HORSE

ALL the principles of riding apply to the longeing as well (028, 029). One needs a well-cultivated eye and an intuitive sense for the horse's motion to influence the horse favourably, and reap the benefit from the longeing work. Merely having the animal twirling around (usually in too fast a rhythm), is at best a very poor form of exercising.

With regard to the adjusting of side reins, there are too many variables, from horse to horse, to make any definite recommendations. A general rule, however, is to end up having the horse's head in the correct position when the horse is trotting 033. It is better to have the side reins a bit too loose than too tight.

For some young horses, during approximately the first three to six weeks of longeing, the head should be adjusted facing slightly to the outside. As the horse learns to balance itself, one can gradually change the bend to the inside (on the circle line). The side reins should be quite long for young horses to allow for the forward and downward stretching at any time.

1) Longeing from the halter or cavasson, without side reins or tack, is used for the following reasons:–
   (a)   The very first longeing sessions for the horse. The animal learns its first obedience; that is, going quietly around the handler on both hands, without hindrance from tack.
   (b)   A method of free-longeing for any horse; to give simple, controlled exercise.
   (c)   Initial re-training for badly spoiled horses.
2) Longeing from cavasson with a bit and side reins:–
   (a)   Establishes the balance, regularity and stability in the gaits.
   (b)   The horse learns that the bit is to be respected. The bit doesn't do anything if he leaves it alone and searches a contact on it. However, if the horse pulls against it, hurting himself, he quickly learns to yield to the pressure from the bit.

062
LONGEING THE RIDER

– The purpose for longeing the rider is:–
   (a)   Rider can concentrate solely on himself.
   (b)   Gain suppleness and independence of individual body parts.
   (c)   Attain the correct position, which is an integral part of the good seat.
   (d)   In keeping with the fact that the driving attitude of the upperbody and seat is that which welds horse and rider together, the pupil should be made to activate the horse, by himself as much as possible. (007)
– Which horse should be used to longe the rider?
   While longeing beginner riders, until they become acquainted with the motion of the horse, and gain confidence in coping with the unfamiliar task of riding, a reliable, quiet, older horse should be used. As the student becomes more proficient, more volatile and energetic horses can be used.

Note. In the first years of training, the young horse should be spared this pounding-around on the longe, with riders doing sitting trot without stirrups.

– Points of caution while longeing:–

- Have the longe line carefully organized (no knots or twirls). If the horse bolts, and the longe line is badly organized, the line can easily knot firmly onto the hand, resulting in broken finger or hand bones.
- Always have the bridle reins tied up in such a way, that the person being longed can use the reins to control the horse if something unforeseen happens (line breaking etc.).

REFLECTIONS VI

- An experienced rider doesn't necessarily need to use severe bits, an inexperienced rider certainly should not use them.
- In the truest sense of the word the bit must remain the mediator between horse and rider, upon which neither may pull (neutral territory).
- The riding school should be a place of quiet work. Excessive noise in either the school or around the stables should be avoided.
- The horse should be tacked up carefully, with proper fitting tack. Carelessness can cause saddle or girth sores, or tossing of the head if bridles are uncomfortable or ill-fitted.
- Tighten the girth gradually, and never over-tighten it, as tensions will be caused in the horse's back.
- Be gentle with the horse while grooming; remember, true horsemanship starts on the ground.
- It is not a praise for the horse to get huge slaps on the neck or croup.
- Beginner riders aren't bad riders. The only truly bad riders are those who blatantly and ignorantly bully their horses about.

Barty. Piaffe. Only through continued judicious exercising in the basics will improvement be realized in this advanced work. Though the quality of the contact is good, and the horse is pleasant in its neck and in expression (accepting), the unquiet tail indicates physical strain as the hindquarter commences to lower and bear more weight.

CHAPTER VII

THE SUBJECT OF PHOTOGRAPHY

063
THE ASSESSMENT OF HORSEMANSHIP IN PHOTOGRAPHY

FOR the experienced eye, a photograph of horse and rider is worth considerably more than a thousand words. Pictures reveal accurately the performance of both horse and rider at the particular moment that the shot was taken.

One should certainly not condemn a rider on the strength of one photograph; everyone has a bad day once in a while. The personal value in assessing equestrian photos lies in establishing more clearly in one's mind what the required standard of Academic horsemanship is, thereby becoming more proficient in criticizing one's own work, and better equipped to improve upon it. To sharpen one's perception for judging pictures, frequent practice is essential.

One should adhere to a set plan of evaluation, to avoid the problem of trying to see everything at once, and ending-up seeing almost nothing at all.

064
SUGGESTED SEQUENCE TO FOLLOW IN ASSESSING PHOTOGRAPHS
    1) General impression.
    2) Technical points.
    3) Purity of gaits.

065

GENERAL IMPRESSION

FAVOURABLE ATTRIBUTES	POOR ATTRIBUTES
Pleasing	A forced appearance
Harmonious	Unbalanced
Balanced	Awkward
Elegant	Generally unpleasant
Beautiful	

The apparent ease of the performance

066

TECHNICAL POINTS

(a) Correct position of the horse's head (033).

(b) Sufficient length in the neck.

(c) Flexion of knee and hock of those legs suspended in the air. (Depends somewhat on the timing of the photo).*

(d) The horse must appear to be in front of the rider.

(e) Flowing tail carriage.

(f) Pleasant, quiet, accepting expression on horse's face.

(g) Correct position and seat of rider (see chapter 2).

(h) The pensive, composed, unforced appearance of the rider.

---

* One should always take into account the individual's build, suppleness and degree of training. A green horse, no matter how well ridden, will simply not look as good as a well trained horse in the medium or advanced stages of dressage. Also, those horses with a round 'Hackney' motion, will generally make far more spectacular photos than those with a more flat 'daisy-cutter' motion. This difference is particularly evident in the collected work.

The timing of the shot is similarly pertinent to making a viable judgement. When taken too late, the front foot will already be on the ground. When taken too soon, the legs will not be extended forward sufficiently to demonstrate the gait to best advantage. Therefore, the photo which is taken correctly, will demonstrate most clearly the amount of flexion of the knee and hock, and also show the amount of leg activity.

PURITY OF THE GAITS

    (a)   Establish which gait is being portrayed.

    (b)   Check the purity of the gait.
- walk, 4-beat (044)
- trot, 2-beat (046)
- canter, 3-beat (047)
- rein-back, 2-beat (052)

    (c)   In extensions, the horse's whole frame must lengthen; the hindlegs following actively and purely.

    (d)   In collection, the horse must appear to be going up-hill because of a supple back which results in a lowered, more engaged hindquarter.

Note: In photographs there is little appreciable visual difference between medium and extended trot because the length of the moment of suspension does not show. At the medium trot the horse will already have almost fully extended its legs. That which differentiates the middle trot from the extended trot lies only in a more powerful thrusting off of the hind legs, resulting in a more pronounced moment of suspension and therefore a longer stride.

At the extended trot the front leg should point to the place where it will be landing; an exaggerated 'forward-upward' reaching of the forelimbs (goose-stepping) should be avoided. Ideally speaking, the front feet should NOT extend beyond the line drawn along the horse's face to the ground. However, some horses do display great freedom of the shoulder and do extend the forelimbs somewhat beyond this line, which is acceptable provided that the requirement of diagonal unison is still fulfilled (046).

Any deviations from the exact, correct footfall must be deemed to be a deviation from the ideal standard of Academic riding.

Plate 29. Meteorite. Extended trot. (May 1977). Here the horse is extending as a young horse would, despite his 13+ years of age (lacking in a correct foundation training). Still relying considerably on the hand for balance, the forehand dives close to the ground.

Plate 56. Meteorite. Extended trot. (May 1978). The forehand is becoming lighter.

Plate 99. Meteorite. Extended trot (Oct. 1978). Shows better freeing of the forehand. Note that with the improvement of the gait (the horse can be balanced more easily because of a more supple back) the rider is able to sit more deeply.

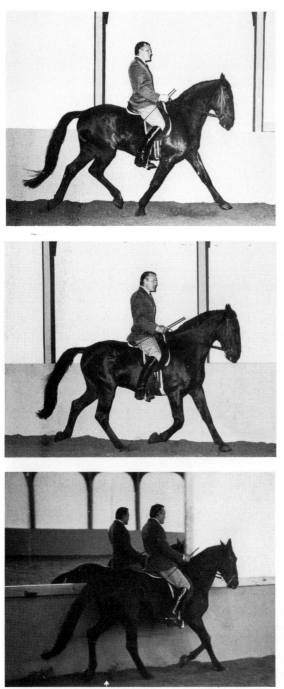

Plate 65. Meteorite. Incorrect work. An over-sped forehand at the extended trot. Note that the right front foot is still on the ground while its diagonal partner (left hind) is already airborne. (See definition of diagonal unison). 046.

Plate 98. Meteorite. Incorrect work. An over-sped hindquarter at the extended trot. The right hind foot has landed long before its diagonal partner, the left front. Such indications of tensions can be shown by any horse that is not supple. One's eye must be very sharply developed to be able to see these points while the horse is in motion. Conveniently, the camera captures this split-second disharmony.

Plate 97. Meteorite. Correct work. A diagonally unified landing at the extended trot. The arrow indicates the place where the right front foot has left the ground.

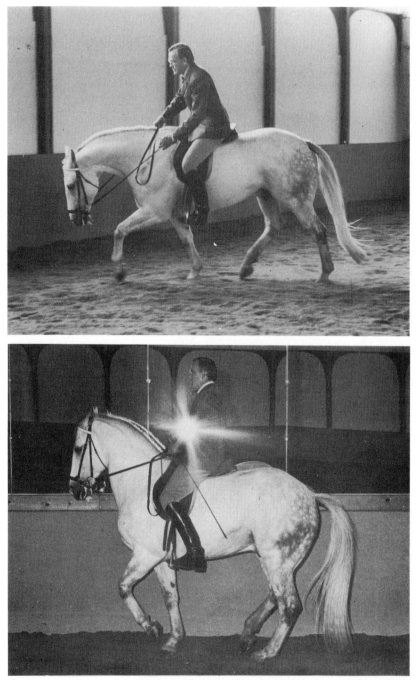

These photos portray Atlantis during Piaffe work. The corner-stone of correct work lies in the presence of the supple back. These photos illustrate this from, on the one hand (top), a soft stretching and yielding forward and down (the horse's nose should be pointing somewhat more forward, see plate on page 48), and on the other hand,

the supple deeply bent haunches in the Piaffe (bottom left). Compare the height of the tail from the ground with plate on page 72. On the right hand page the horse is shown in a more advanced (though still unfinished) stage of the training, both in a snaffle and in a double bridle.

068

INCORRECT WORK

INCORRECT work invariably manifests itself in the distortion of the gaits, usually because of either laziness or tensions. In both instances the horse doesn't step through its back.

LAZINESS: The horse may seem quite happy and the general appearance pleasant, however, one will be able to detect a lagging hindquarter and imbalance within the horse which drags itself about on the forehand, often boring on the rider's hands, sometimes with the face behind the vertical.

TENSIONS: Almost without exception, tensions start in the horse's back, then manifest themselves in the poll and jaw and in the stiff tail carriage. As a result the horses no longer flex the joints in their legs, and go around 'peg-legged'; using their legs only, without the cooperation of a supple, elastic back. (Such horses are referred to as 'leg-goers'.)

069

THE SIGNS OF TENSIONS OR INCORRECT WORK

- Incorrect head position of the horse (033).
- Too short a neck, in relation to the degree of extension or collection of the gait.
- The croup is high; the horse appears to be out behind the rider.
- Impure footfall in the gaits. The legs appear stiff.
- Crookedness
- Tensions visible in the neck, poll or jaw.
- Horse's neck broken or 'kinked' at the third vertebra behind the poll.
- The tail carriage is stiff or swishing.
- The horse's mouth is dry. The lips are opened, snarling.
- The angry, unhappy or frightened expression on the horse's face and eyes.

- Poor position of the rider. (See Chapter II, and 019, 020).
- Any stiffness detected in the rider.
- Rider does not appear to be sitting IN the horse; a general picture of disharmony and discomfort.
- Rider's facial expression strained.

CONCLUSION

Few people would refute that it is a most splendid sight to observe horses out in the pasture, cavorting about at play, expressing their exuberant spirit in motion. The fine riding of an experienced horseman can be just as fascinating to watch and is visibly a pleasure for both rider and mount, who do not show the hard years of disciplined work, but rather the fruit thereof . . . a harmony and lightness, pesented with playful ease.

To realize these ideals, great care must be taken in laying down the foundations of riding upon the solid bedrock of proven equestrian principles. However, the finest of theory is of little value without the assistance of an experienced person to act as translator; mediating between horse and rider. This guidance cannot be fulfilled by merely expounding an anthology of fanciful theories which are devotedly recommended but never substantiated in practice. Pertinent demonstrations from the saddle are an indispensable factor in the learning process, showing examples of work which is in sympathy with the horse's nature and concurs with the standards of Academic Riding.

The horses will remain the pure and ultimate judges, let us always listen to them.

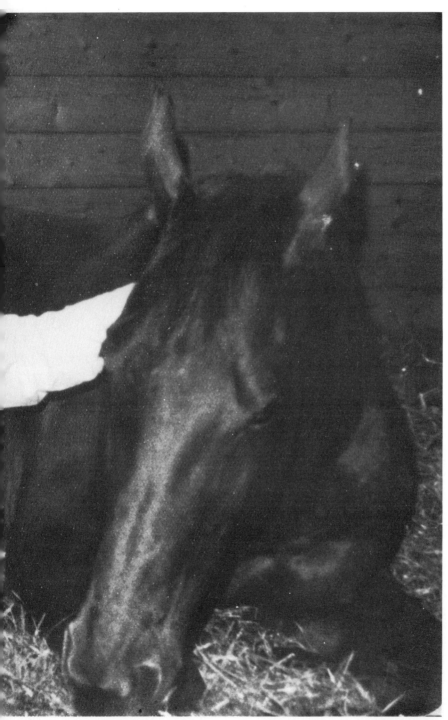

PHOTO BY J.G. HERBERMANN

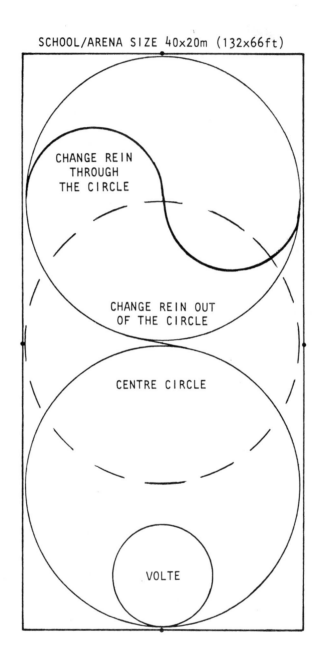

CHANGE REIN
THROUGH
THE CIRCLE

CHANGE REIN OUT
OF THE CIRCLE

CENTRE CIRCLE

VOLTE

108

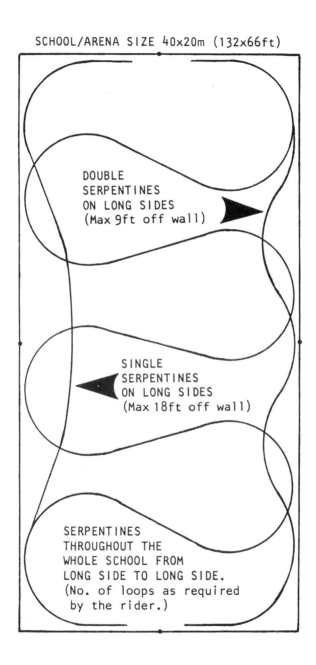

SCHOOL/ARENA SIZE 40x20m (132x66ft)

DOUBLE
SERPENTINES
ON LONG SIDES
(Max 9ft off wall)

SINGLE
SERPENTINES
ON LONG SIDES
(Max 18ft off wall)

SERPENTINES
THROUGHOUT THE
WHOLE SCHOOL FROM
LONG SIDE TO LONG SIDE.
(No. of loops as required
by the rider.)

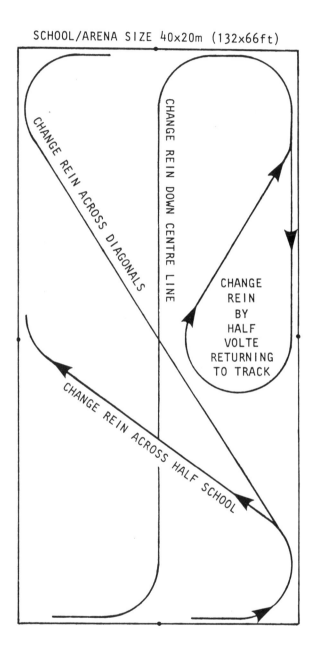

SCHOOL/ARENA SIZE 40x20m (132x66ft)

CHANGE REIN ACROSS DIAGONALS

CHANGE REIN DOWN CENTRE LINE

CHANGE REIN BY HALF VOLTE RETURNING TO TRACK

CHANGE REIN ACROSS HALF SCHOOL

SCHOOL/ARENA SIZE 40x20m (132x66ft)

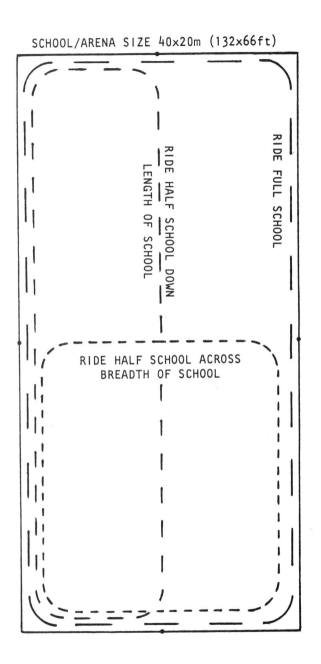

RIDE FULL SCHOOL

RIDE HALF SCHOOL DOWN
LENGTH OF SCHOOL

RIDE HALF SCHOOL ACROSS
BREADTH OF SCHOOL